# INFORMATION MARKETING

# INFORMATION MARKETING

Jennifer Rowley

# Ashgate

Aldershot • Burlington USA • Singapore • Sydney

Published by
Ashgate Publishing Limited
Gower House
Croft Road
Aldershot
Hants GU11 3HR
England

Ashgate Publishing Company
131 Main Street
Burlington VT 05401-5600 USA

Jennifer Rowley has asserted her right under the Copyright, Designs and Patents Act 1988 to be identified as the author of this work.

British Library Cataloguing in Publication Data
Rowley, J. E. (Jennifer E.), 1950–
Information marketing
1. Information services – Marketing
I. Title
025′.00688

Library of Congress Control Number: 2001088794

ISBN 0 566 08222 5

Typeset in 10pt Century Old Style by Intype London Ltd, Wimbledon and printed in Great Britain by MPG Books Ltd, Bodmin, Cornwall.

# Contents

# List of figures

# Acknowledgements

I am indebted to a wide range of authors who have explored and developed frameworks and models for thinking about marketing. My interest in marketing was 'caught' in my days in the Department of Business and Management Studies in the Crewe and Alsager Faculty at Manchester Metropolitan University. Marketing is contagious, and entirely consistent with my longstanding interest in strategies for improving the effective and efficient use of information. I caught marketing from Ruth Ashford, Jill Dawes and Peter Jones. I am grateful for many wide-ranging discussions with these people and others in the Department of Retailing and Marketing at the Manchester Metropolitan University, who have at times been patient with my ignorance. As for the information marketplace, my contacts with players in that field over many years, as tutor, interested observer and commentator, researcher, consultant and practising professional are too many to mention. I hope that they will regard this book as a worthwhile contribution to the debate. On a personal note, my daughters, Shula and Zeta, who, as small children, were acknowledged in my earlier books because without their accommodation the books would never have been written, are now complaining that they have not seen their names in print for some while. These days their contributions are different. As I complete this manuscript, Shula is cooking Sunday dinner, and Zeta is writing a story in her bedroom.

# Acknowledgements

# Introduction

Technologically led developments are changing the nature of the information marketplace. In the face of rapid change, stakeholders and players in that marketplace need to form new strategic alliances, identify new market segments, evolve new products, and, in general, manage changing relationships between suppliers and customers. If organizations in the information marketplace are to survive and flourish, they need to be confident about their mission and role, and to be continually alert to technological, economic, political and social factors that are reshaping the context in which they seek to serve users, contribute to communities, attract and retain customers, and establish and maintain relationships with other organizations.

In such an environment, suppliers need to employ the full armoury of marketing concepts, approaches and tactics. At the heart of marketing practice and theory is the 'marketing concept'. An organization that embraces the marketing concept 'tries to provide products that satisfy customer needs though a co-ordinated set of activities that also allow the organization to achieve its goals. Customer satisfaction is the major aim of the marketing concept' (Dibb et al., 1994, p. 11). The marketing concept should affect all areas and activities of the organization and not just promotional activities, or those activities performed through the marketing department. Marketing needs to permeate the organization; it should influence operational, tactical and strategic decision-making and actions.

This book takes as its focus 'information marketing'. We define information marketing as 'the marketing of information-based products and services' and focus on marketing in contexts and organizations in which information-based products and services are a significant product category. Typical information-based products include books, CDs, videos, journals, journal articles, databases, electronic journals, newspapers and databanks. Typical information-based services include public libraries, academic libraries, workplace information centres, access to databases, electronic current-awareness services, business consultancy services, subject gateways, and Web-based information services. Libraries, bookshops, database producers, online search services, business intelligence services and portals act as the interface between the consumer and the producer in respect of these products. Within the marketplace there are also a host of other organizations that often interact with the consumer through one of these 'retailers'. These organizations are important in business-to-business transactions within the marketplace, but in a changing marketplace their relationship with consumers may become more direct. Examples are interlibrary loans service providers, national libraries, publishers and library consortia. A major theme of commentaries on e-commerce is the potential for disintermediation in all e-marketplaces; the role of the intermediary is being reassessed. Intermediaries in e-marketplaces will survive if they 'add value' to the product offering in a way that is not available from the manufacturer, producer, or wholesaler. In order to explore the traditional ways in which 'retailers' such as libraries have added-value, and the continued relevance of their role in the information marketplace, it is necessary to investigate the nature of information products more fully. Chapter 5 explores the concept of information products. For the purpose of defining the scope of this book, the emphasis is on the interface between the consumer and the information provider, and in this much attention is directed to the role of library and information services. However, in considering both the marketing strategies and activities undertaken by these organizations and the changing nature of information products and the information marketplace, it is important not to neglect the roles of other organizations in that marketplace.

This book, then, seeks to make a contribution to thinking about marketing by managers and marketers in a wide range of organizations. Some of these organizations will have dedicated marketing departments, whilst others will have only part-time marketers. Some are in the public sector, and are a part of another organization, whilst others are significant commercial concerns in their own right. In seeking to bridge this wide spectrum of organizational sophistication in relation to marketing, the book draws together ideas that challenge all such organizations to reflect on the nature of their product, their relationships with customers, and the changing landscape of the information marketplace. The overarching approach of the text is designed to encourage marketing thinking that will link different levels of previous involvement with marketing activities. For those less well acquainted with marketing who would welcome practical advice and ideas, figures giving 'practical tips' are included throughout. Reflection points here and there offer opportunities to reflect on ideas and apply them in the reader's own context. These could be used to focus individual reflection or as the basis for group discussion.

The book is divided into ten chapters. Early chapters explore basic concepts such as the nature of marketing and the structure of the information marketplace. Chapters 1 and 2 encourage the reader to focus on customers and their relationships with them. Chapter 3 explores different customer groups, segmentation, and the factors that influence consumer behaviour. Chapter 4 looks at the building of customer relationships, taking into account topics such as the service experience and customer loyalty. Chapter 5 considers information as a product. Another dimension of the offering, the brand and corporate identity, is discussed in Chapter 6. Marketing communications (Chapter 7) is concerned with promotion of the organization and/or its products. Price (Chapter 8) is an important element in the marketing mix. Chapter 9 explores approaches to collecting customer data. Finally, Chapter 10 demonstrates how all these elements can be drawn together in marketing strategy and planning.

This book's unique perspective will make it of interest to students and professionals involved in the information marketplace. Specifically, this includes students on undergraduate and postgraduate courses in information management, library and information studies, business information technology, marketing, e-commerce and communication studies. The information marketplace is international; hence this text is not constrained by national or cultural boundaries.

## REFERENCE

Dibb, S., Simkin, L., Pride, W.M. and Ferrell, O.C. (1994), *Marketing Concepts and Strategies*. 2nd European edition. Boston and London: Houghton Mifflin.

# 1 Marketing

## AIMS

This chapter sets the scene for the remainder of the book by introducing a number of key marketing concepts, and by explaining how the elements of marketing practice that are discussed in greater depth in the chapters that follow can be drawn together to inform marketing strategy. This chapter introduces:

- definitions of marketing, and the concept of marketing orientation; and
- the marketing mix.

## INTRODUCTION

Organizations and professionals in the information marketplace have a wide range of prior levels of experience with marketing. These experiences, gathered in both professional and consumer roles, will colour their reactions. Responses to marketing fall into two groups, typified by the following statements:

1. Marketing is concerned with encouraging people to buy things that they don't really need or want, and interfering with people's behaviours, attitudes and values, or
2. Marketing is designed to bring you the products you want, when you want them, where you want them, at prices you can afford, and with the information that is necessary to make informed and satisfying customer choices.

Most people could cite examples of marketing that fit both of these descriptions. Aggressive marketing tactics pursued by some of the organizations in the consumer marketplace have had a major influence on what we eat, what we wear, how we spend our leisure time, and a host of other dimensions of our social and cultural experience. In addition, privatization and corresponding marketization of the public sector in recent years have justifiably made employees in the public sector, in sectors such as education and public libraries, sceptical as to the relevance and impact of marketing in these environments. Unquestionably, there are ethical issues associated with marketing. It is, after all, designed to influence, and where there are significant commercial gains at stake, high-profile advertising campaigns can be very attractive. Yet this very statement is merely a confirmation of the importance of marketing in our society. The position taken in this book is consistent with the concept of marketing orientation which will be explored later in this chapter; that is, marketing's role is communicating with and understanding customers, and responding to customer needs.

Two widely used definitions are a useful starting point in exploring the various aspects of marketing as both an activity and a philosophy:

1. 'Marketing is the management process which identifies, anticipates, and supplies customer requirements efficiently and profitably' (Chartered Institute of Marketing).
2. 'Marketing is the process of planning and executing the conception, pricing, promotion and distribution of ideas, goods and services to create, exchange and satisfy individual and organizational objectives' (American Marketing Association).

These definitions embed a number of key aspects of marketing:

First, marketing is a **business process**, and as such needs to be executed, which requires time and resources. Larger organizations have dedicated marketing departments that take responsibility for managing and executing elements of the marketing function. Such departments have a responsibility for understanding the marketplace in which the organization operates, and can act as an interface between other departments in an organization and the external environment. In organizations in which there is no specialist marketing function, responsibility for marketing still needs to rest somewhere in the organization.

*REFLECT: Who takes responsibility for the marketing function in your organization?*

Second, marketing is about **meeting customer requirements**. All marketing activities should be customer focused. Customer requirements need to be understood and met, using the resources at the disposal of the organization. These organizational resources define the product offering that the organization is in a position to make to the customer. They constrain the market in which the organization can function, but within these constraints the organization must tailor the resources and the use of resources to meet the needs of an appropriate customer group. Often, meeting customer requirements means anticipating those requirements, such as when new products are launched or new customer groups are courted.

Third, marketing **meets the organization's objectives** by assisting the organization to fulfil customer requirements efficiently and profitably. Efficient use of resources is important to success in both profit and non-profit sectors. Most businesses exist to create a profit, but where this is not a key objective, as in some public sector situations, there is still a need to control costs and adhere to budgets, and generally maintain the financial health of the organization.

Fourth, marketing is **an exchange process**, which may be very straightforward. The organization offers a product or a service, and the customer offers a sum of money in return. For example, if you want to buy a book, you establish that the bookseller has a book to offer, and you browse it to assess whether you are interested in its content, and then pay for it. In other situations the exchange process may be a little less obvious. So, for example, citizens pay taxes to support public library services. In exchange they expect to be able to access quick reference services and leisure reading, among other facilities. Exchange processes do not always have to involve money. A volunteer may give time, and political parties are interested in securing votes. Both parties must *value* what the other is offering. This reciprocated value is the basis for customer satisfaction and further exchanges. Repeated exchanges can lead to what marketers describe as a relationship between the customer and the supplier. The concept of relationships is explored more fully in Chapter 4.

Fifth, marketing **applies to ideas, goods and services**, referred to by the generic term 'product'. However, the dominance of goods marketing in the consumer marketplace has led to a popular usage in which the terms goods and products tend to be treated as synonymous, and so it is often necessary to make explicit reference to the service component in a product offering. Ideas are promoted by political parties and pressure groups, whose aim is to change attitudes and beliefs. Goods include any physical objects that can be exchanged; services include personal services, such as hairdressing, retailing, and professional services, such as information services, accountancy and legal advice. As we shall discuss further in Chapter 5, many product offerings comprise a complex mixture of goods, services, ideas, and possibly information, if this can be regarded as distinct from the other three product types.

*REFLECT: Describe some other exchange processes relevant to the information industry; who are the two parties, and what do they give to each other?*

The organization that develops and uses its understanding of customer requirements to shape its activities and strategy has a **marketing orientation**. This is a philosophy that places customers and their needs at the heart of what the organization does. The assumption is that customers are looking for the offering that best fits their needs, and therefore the organization must define those needs and develop appropriate offerings. These offerings include product, brand, price, delivery options and any other relevant elements of the **marketing mix** (see below). Customers are individuals, and each person's or organization's needs may be different. In order to respond in an efficient way, organizations define customer groups, and seek to meet the needs that can be associated with those groups. If organizations do not create and hold customers, clients, users, or members, they undermine the reason for their existence.

When expressed in these terms, marketing orientation may seem the obvious way forward. Businesses have only embraced marketing orientation relatively recently. Other options are:

- **Production orientation**, where the emphasis is on making products that are affordable and available; price is seen as the differentiating factor between products, and customers are assumed to buy the cheapest product.
- **Product orientation**, where the focus is on quality of the product, and consumers are assumed to seek the highest level of quality for their money.
- **Sales orientation**, where the assumption is that consumers are reluctant to purchase, and therefore need encouragement, and products are pushed towards them.

    REFLECT: Taking an organization that is familiar to you, describe the impact that these different business and marketing philosophies might have on that organization.

Marketing orientation should sit comfortably with the traditional public service ethos in which there was a concern for user needs. There is, however, an ever-present danger that information services may slip back into an approach that is more sales oriented. The enormous resources and archives held by libraries, and the backlists held by publishers, are inclined to encourage such organizations to sell their resources or products to the public, rather than clinging to a true marketing orientation. In addition, the speed of technologically led change in the information industry is inclined to encourage either a production orientation or a selling orientation. Figure 1.1 demonstrates the implications of a marketing orientation for one public library.

## THE MARKETING MIX

The marketing mix is the combination of four major tools of marketing – product, price, promotion and place – known widely as the 4Ps. The marketing mix is an important tool for creating and maintaining an offering that is of value to customers. Before the elements in the marketing mix can be discussed and

Our library is 'user-centred' and is organized to this end over administrative ease. Not for us separate reference and lending libraries, but subject libraries with teams qualified professionally, academically and by experience to promote their subjects throughout the town. That is their remit – they buy and organize stock, answer questions, give advice and do the traditional work of a librarian and information officer, but they also organize lectures, seminars and other live activities relating to their subject; they conceive and organize exhibitions; they write press releases; they compose advertising copy; they vie with each other to produce stimulating activities to persuade the community to use library facilities. They are so successful that we claim to be the busiest library system in London . . .

We have decided to 'bring the library into the marketplace'. Not for us the off-putting image of a reserved academic backwater – although there are quiet places of study, and our subject departments serve our users in depth. Rather we have embraced the décor of a good department store embellished with the exciting but paradoxical ordinariness of a street market. We actually use market stalls and our gallery display space is filled with a succession of ever-changing activities – art exhibitions, booksales, computer fairs, craft demonstrations, jazz concerts, music recitals, etc. We have let the space for the sale of encyclopaedias, gas stoves, showers, timeshares and holidays. Our coffee shop is never empty and our book, jigsaw and souvenir sales produce a healthy profit, and add to the spirit of the place. We attract people and we pride ourselves in catering for their needs. My staff are always searching for new and improved services, ranging from major activities like online services to small but still important adjuncts to the service such as umbrella loans (good advertising); the Domesday Discs; facilities for nursing mothers, etc. You can buy a ticket for a show, hire a typewriter or a market stall; consult a book or periodical or listen to records and cassettes . . . Talks to some kind of local society are a weekly occurrence. Posters advertising our activities are everywhere. Our relationship with the press is a busy strand of our marketing plan. We are blessed with four very good series of local newspapers and we certainly cultivate them . . . Consequently we are rarely out of the headlines . . .

*Source:* extracted from R. Smith, 'Marketing the library', in *Marketing of Library and Information Services*, ed. Blaise Cronin. London: Aslib, 1992, pp. 123–4.

**Figure 1.1** On being marketing oriented

explored, the organization must undertake a range of processes in order to identify customer needs. One valuable source of such information is customers' responses to current product offerings, which will be evident from sales level, customer surveys, complaints and other channels through which the organization listens to its customers. Other data may be collected on customers' attitudes to potential new products, or to communication messages, or to competitors' products. A number of chapters in this book explore aspects of understanding customers. Chapter 3 examines the segmentation of customer populations and consumer decision-making behaviour. Chapter 4 looks at customer relationships. Chapter 9 discusses approaches to collecting and managing customer data through marketing research activities and marketing information systems.

Returning to the marketing mix, successful marketing depends on 'the right mix'. In other words, a product that lacks visibility among the potential customer group will fail; a marketing message that evidently does not reflect the product will suffer the same fate. All elements of the marketing mix are interdependent, and must be consistent with one another. The most appropriate marketing mix depends upon the customer and is influenced by the marketing environment. An organization needs to design and combine elements of the marketing mix so as to create an offering that differentiates it from its competitors, or to create a competitive advantage.

The elements of the marketing mix can be changed. However, most such changes are constrained by the organization's existing resources (including its existing customer base), and the rate of change that is possible may at times be too slow. For example, libraries often occupy specific buildings; location may be a significant aspect of distribution, yet it is often difficult to alter except in the long term.

There have been many proposals to extend the original 4Ps. The most useful of these is Booms and Bitner's (1981) proposal that in order to characterize the marketing mix for services, the 4Ps should be extended to 7Ps to include people, processes and physical evidence. Since most products include both goods and service elements, we describe each of these 7Ps briefly below:

- **Product** is the aspect of the marketing mix that deals with the creation, development and management of products. Product decisions are important because they directly involve creating products that satisfy customers' needs and wants. An organization must maintain a satisfactory set of products; this involves introducing new products, modifying existing ones and eliminating those that no longer satisfy customers and/or yield acceptable profits. Chapter 5 explores the nature of information products, emphasizing their functionality. Products also have psychological benefits (which encourage people to own them or to participate in a service interaction or community). These are to some extent encapsulated in the brand, which is discussed in Chapter 6.
- **Price** relates to activities associated with establishing pricing objectives and strategies and determining product prices. It defines the value obtained in an exchange. It may be used as a competitive tool and is one of the marketing mix variables that can be altered relatively quickly to respond to changes in the environment. Price plays both an economic and a psychological role. From an economic perspective price is closely associated with costs and profits. From a psychological perspective, it may be used as an indicator of quality. In the service sector, the psychological role of price is magnified because consumers must rely on it as the sole indicator of service quality: the intangible nature of services means that other quality indicators are absent.
- **Place** Products must be available at the right time and at a convenient location. Place is concerned both with consumer service delivery points such

as retail outlets and libraries and with the distribution network that ensures that products make their way from the producer or creator to the user or consumer. Delivery channels are significant factors within an industry and involve a complex web of organizational relationships, in which collaboration and competition are equally important. Dimensions of these issues are explored in Chapter 2, which discusses the structure and nature of the information marketplace.

Distribution involves making products available in sufficient quantities to satisfy as many customers as possible, and keeping the total inventory, transport and storage costs as low as possible. Distribution, in the sense of offering the right service at the right time and in a convenient location, is particularly important for services, where value may be viewed as transient. Libraries, both academic and public, are usually situated close to their target market, occupying central locations on university campuses and in city centres or shopping centres. The chief difficulty arises from the fact that some of these locations were chosen over fifty years ago, and may no longer be central to the target market. Additional branch libraries and mobile libraries may seek to alleviate this situation, but do not offer a complete solution. Electronic delivery of documents and information offer availability at the desktop in the home or the office. Mobile technology is starting to allow delivery to whatever location the person occupies.

- **Promotion** relates to activities used to inform one or more groups of people about an organization and its products. It can be used more generally to increase public awareness of an organization and of new or existing products, or alternatively, to educate consumers about product features, or to maintain public awareness of existing products. Promotion includes advertising, public relations, personal selling and direct marketing. It is one element of the two-way communication with customers that forms the basis for customer relationships.

  Promotion of services presents specific difficulties because they are intangible. It is difficult to depict the intangible in advertising, so service advertising needs to emphasize tangible clues, such as physical facilities or other concepts that project an image that reflects services. Personal selling can be powerful in services because this form of promotion allows customers and sales persons to interact. Customer contact personnel therefore have an important promotional function.

- **People** Most services use people in service delivery, often creating and delivering the product in interaction with the customer. The quality of the interaction between the service agent and the customer has a major influence on satisfaction. In services where the level of contact is high, as in dentistry or physiotherapy, the customer needs to feel comfortable with the service

7

agent, to trust them, and to develop a rapport with them, probably over a service relationship that comprises several episodes. Even where the service is less intimate, as in a shop or a library, the attitude and responsiveness of the staff can make a difference to the acceptability of the service experience. The service experience and relationships are discussed in Chapter 4.

- **Process** Services are manufactured and consumed live, and because they involve an interaction between two people, it is more difficult to exercise control and ensure consistency. Marketers, together with managers, need to design the service process carefully. This can include queuing arrangements, processing customer details and payment, as well as elements of the core service delivery. Thus call centre operators and help lines may have a standard set of questions that they ask each caller, and dentist's practice will have a standard approach to receiving patients, calling them into the surgery, and giving treatment. Once a customer has experienced a service process for the first time, they start to learn what their contribution to the process should be, or to 'learn the script'; this helps them to feel more comfortable with the process. In self-service environments, for example a public access kiosk, the customer is taken through a process by the prompts on the computer screen.

- **Physical evidence** is concerned with the physical surroundings from which a service is delivered and other tangible elements in a service episode (such as cutlery, table napkins, and shampoo in a hotel). Physical evidence is important in service delivery, because it is usually the only tangible clue that the customer has about the quality of the service experience. Thus hotels, hospitals, universities and leisure resorts must pay attention to atmosphere, ambience, image and the design of premises.

*REFLECT: Discuss the physical evidence that customers encounter in your organization. What messages does this evidence communicate about the organization and the products it offers?*

## CONCLUSION

All information providers are concerned with customer satisfaction. A powerful philosophy to assist an organization in giving customer satisfaction is marketing orientation. This involves identifying customer needs and requirements and then seeking to meet those needs. Marketers use the marketing mix to consider aspects of the offering that they make to customers. The 7Ps of this marketing mix are product, price, place, promotion, people, process and physical evidence.

# REFERENCES AND FURTHER READING

Adcock, D., Bradfield, R., Halborg, A. and Ross, C. (1998), *Marketing Principles and Practice*. 3rd edition. London: Pitman Publishing.

Baker, M.J. (1991), *Marketing: An Introductory Text*. 5th edition (1994 reprint). London: Macmillan.

Baker, M. (ed.) (1995), *Marketing: Theory and Practice*. 3rd edition. London: Macmillan.

Bateson, J.E.G. (1995), *Managing Services Marketing: Text and Readings*. 3rd edition. Fort Worth, TX and London: Dryden Press.

Booms, B.H. and Bitner, M.J. (1981), 'Marketing strategies and organization structures for service firms', in *Marketing of Services*, eds J. Donnelly and W.R. George. American Marketing Association.

Dibb, S., Simkin, L., Pride, W.M. and Ferrell, O.C. (1994), *Marketing Concepts and Strategies*. 2nd European edition. Boston, MA and London: Houghton Mifflin.

Gabbott, M. and Hogg, G. (1997), *Contemporary Service Marketing Management: A Reader*. London: Dryden Press.

Hoffman, K.D. and Bateson, K.E.G. (1997), *The Essentials of Services Marketing*. Fort Worth, TX: Dryden Press.

Hutchings, A. (1995), *Marketing: A Resource Book*. London: Pitman.

Kotler, P. (1994), *Marketing Management: Analysis, Planning, Implementation and Control*. 8th edition. London: Prentice Hall International.

Lovelock, C.H. (1996), *Services Marketing*. 3rd edition. New Jersey and London: Prentice Hall.

Mercer, D. (1996), *Marketing*. 2nd edition. Oxford: Blackwell.

# 2 The information marketplace

## AIMS

This chapter encourages reflection on the context in which customers and information providers interact, first by profiling aspects of the information marketplace, and then by considering aspects of the marketing environment for that marketplace. Key areas explored include:

- the nature of information as a product;
- customers;
- profiling the information industry; and
- the marketing environment.

## INTRODUCTION

> For any company to command a strategic business posture towards the EP [electronic publishing] business, it must have an understanding of the EP role in books, periodicals and newspaper publishing; in corporate, financial and bibliographic services; in the computer, consumer electronic, TV, cable and telecommunications sectors.
> (Blunden and Blunden, 1994, p. 6)

Although the above quotation relates specifically to the electronic publishing industry, it is equally applicable to the knowledge industry in general. The powerful point embedded in this quote is the breadth of the industry. The knowledge industry embraces both electronic and print products, and a range of organizations with different roles and market niches. Whilst the Internet and associated electronic information sources are important new entrants to the information marketplace, the traditional print marketplace remains significant. Indeed, information products such as books and CD-ROMs represent a significant category of products in e-retailing ventures. Hybrid libraries that manage access to a collection of networked information resources, as well as a collection of print resources, will appeal to users for the foreseeable future. The roles of all stakeholders in the information marketplace are undergoing revision, and the library and its staff are no exception. In some arenas, services previously provided by libraries are being superseded by access to electronic information resources through the Internet. On the other hand, the wider availability of information resources over the Internet may heighten awareness of information and create a more discerning public which both recognizes the central value of information and is more discriminating in its use of information. Exposure to a wealth of information to the extent of overload is likely to provoke a sharpened perception of the quality of structure and guidance in knowledge bases, and demand for powerful search engines.

Marketplace issues play a significant role in determining access to information and the role that information professionals play in facilitating such access. What is the electronic information marketplace? Schwuchow (1995, p. 123) warns that:

> the very definition of the information sector is in flux. It is, indeed, very difficult to define this sector of economic activity because of the dramatic development in the technologies and all of the recent mergers in the entertainment, telecommunications and information industries.

Nevertheless it is important that information professionals understand key characteristics of this marketplace, however elusive and changing its boundaries might be. The opportunities offered by enhanced electronic information and communication systems have affected the way in which businesses operate; they also affect both internal communication and communication with suppliers and customers in the arena of e-business. The application of such systems also fuels the drive towards a knowledge-based society. All parties in the information industry are on the front line of such changes. Whilst in other organizations effective knowledge management may be a means to an end or an internal product that supports staff in achieving organizational objectives, the primary product of most of the players in the information industry is knowledge management, either in the form of a service, such as information management consultancy or library service, or as a product that provides packaged information, for example in a database or a printed directory.

Product and service quality are usually defined in terms of meeting the customer's needs; the importance of analysing more carefully the structure of the marketplace for information is evident. Each organization in the information marketplace must develop a more acute awareness of the needs of its specific client group and, correspondingly, develop a unique portfolio of services. It will no longer be sufficient, for example, to assume that because one library system is providing a given service successfully, that service will work elsewhere. Whilst initiatives will clearly be informed by the contributions of others in the marketplace, and in this context the marketplace is increasingly international, 'me-too' services must be a thing of the past.

Key factors in determining the character of any marketplace are the nature of the product, the customer base and the competitive profile of the marketplace, that is the size of players and their basis for competition. Subsequent chapters develop several of these themes more fully. Chapter 5 encourages reflection on the nature of the information product. Chapter 3 explores customers and their behaviour, and the segmentation of customer markets with the aim of better understanding and responding to customer needs. Approaches to understanding industry structures are revisited in Chapter 10, in the context of marketing strategy. This chapter also reviews other factors that characterize the information marketplace, and reviews aspects of the marketing environment.

## INFORMATION AS A PRODUCT

The product is at the heart of the marketing exchange. Customers buy products to solve problems or to enhance their lives. The product must deliver the benefits that the customer wants, and the ability of the organization to deliver the right product is the ultimate test of whether the organization has understood and responded to its customers' needs. This, in turn, influences its success, either as a public sector service or as a business entity. We use the definition of a product as offered by Brassington and Pettitt (1997, p. 254):

> A product is a physical good, service, idea, person or place that is capable of offering tangible and intangible attributes that individuals or organizations regard as so necessary, worthwhile or satisfying that they are prepared to exchange money, patronage or some other unit of value in order to acquire it.

Aspects of this definition will be further explored in the next chapter, but for the moment it is useful to note the wide definition of 'product' as the entity at the core of any marketing exchange between a customer or user and an organization. In particular, it is important to note that products include both tangible goods (such as books and baked beans), and services (such as information services and hairdressing).

The departure point for this book is that information as a product has a range of unique features that affect the nature of the relationship between customers and information providers, and the nature of the information marketplace. Although Chapter 5 will explore the nature of information as a product in greater detail, it is useful to note at this stage some of the distinguishing characteristics of information as a product before proceeding to consider other aspects of the marketplace. These characteristics are as follows:

- Information as a product is distinct from any other product.
- Information is not only a product, but something that can be used to promote products and to influence individuals.
- Information products take a variety of different forms.

## THE DISTINCT NATURE OF INFORMATION AS A PRODUCT

Central to an understanding of the information marketplace is the recognition that information is neither a good or a service, and that the exchange of information is different from the exchange of other commodities. Eaton and Bawden (1991) summarize some of the special characteristics of information:

- Information is not lost when it is given or sold to others. Boulding (1968) gives an appropriate example: 'When a teacher teaches a class, at the end of an hour the pupils know more, and the teacher usually knows more as well.'
- The value of information is not readily quantifiable. Information has no intrinsic value, and value depends upon context and user.

Additional factors that influence the marketing of electronic information include:

- Information can have multiple lifecycles, as ideas and authors move in and out of fashion (Cronin and Gudim, 1986).
- Technology facilitates and constrains the delivery of information. It is crucial to delivery.
- Demonstration for, say, marketing purposes may involve revealing the information, and thus the exchange may be made before the contract has been agreed.
- Information may be acquired, as with purchase or lease of a CD-ROM or accessed, as with access to Internet resources.
- Information may be repackaged in very many different ways.

## INFORMATION IN PROMOTION AND SOCIETY

The significance of information in a range of applications derives from its intimate connection with communication. Communication is at the core of promotion of products. Thus, for example, a multimedia kiosk that provides evaluated consumer information on gardening products and plants might be made available to customers in a garden centre to help them in the selection of products. Such information is valuable beyond the immediate context of the purchase; in making a purchase the consumer not only gathers information to support the decision-making embedded in the purchase process, but also learns more about the product and aspects of the application in which the product is used. In non-commercial contexts, communities use information in education, and within the public sector to ensure the smooth operation of hospitals and other community services; information can affect the effectiveness and efficiency with which such services can be delivered. Government policy is informed by a range of demographic and economic statistical data. In a knowledge-based society and economy, states and organizations will seek to use knowledge to competitive advantage. In summary, not all information is distributed as a product or, in other words, is available in the public arena and can be purchased. Some is not available for a variety of reasons, and other information is distributed free to the end-consumer.

## RANGE OF INFORMATION PRODUCTS

Information is packaged into a range of print and electronic products – into documents, such as books, CD-ROMs, videos, newspapers, directories and journals. Both consumers and libraries, and other organizations, then purchase and collect such documents. Consumers make these purchases because they intend to use an individual document, libraries make purchases in anticipation of use by one or more of their clients.

Often the same basic data may be packaged in more than one format to meet the requirements of different market segments. Thus many encyclopedias are available in print, Web-based and CD-ROM format. The various versions are not identical: the electronic format might, for example, include additional articles and video clips which cannot be featured in the print format, and certainly the approaches to searching and navigating in the two products will be different. Encyclopedias are an example of a product that may be available in different versions for different audiences, with the possibility of a children's version as well as the full (adult) version. Pricing arrangements may be on a different basis, and there may be different price ranges for different versions of the same product. Newspapers are available in both print form and through Web access. Whilst distribution channels are different, with print newspapers being sold through bookstalls and news-stands and Web-based versions requiring access to a computer workstation, the nature of the product in terms of the benefits that can be derived is also different. The Web-based version of a newspaper can be personalized, and may include added-value services and access to an archive of the newspaper.

The examples used in the discussion above all relate to documents. A document is a knowledge package that:

- has been designed (in terms of style, level and content) for a specific audience (such as students studying GCSE Chemistry, chemical engineers, or researchers in chemistry);
- has been structured at both the micro (detailed structure of text and graphics) and macro (chapter structure and index) levels to support navigation and comprehension.

A range of different types of information services (also products in their own right) structure and package information into forms that suit their audiences. Some of these services, such as market research services and management consultancy, couple information and advice, drawing on both implicit and explicit knowledge, and specialize in providing tailored information to organizations. Other information services rely more heavily on published information that is in the public domain, and assist information and document users in the location of information to assist in decision-making, learning and knowledge acquisition. Amongst such services are those offered by public, academic and workplace libraries and information consultants. Document delivery services are one type of information service that specializes in making documents available to users. They are discussed in more detail below as a means of illustrating the links between the stakeholders in the information industry.

Some examples of products and services that come within the scope of the information industry are given in Figure 2.1. This is in no sense intended to be a comprehensive catalogue of such products, but merely serves to illustrate the diversity of the products in this industry. Attempts to generate comprehensive lists of products are frustrated by difficulties in defining the boundaries of the information industry (and, indeed, the wisdom associated with defining those boundaries differently for different purposes) and keeping up with continual product innovation.

In addition to the goods and services which might be used by individuals and organizations to extend their knowledge base as discussed above, there are many other products embedded in the supply chain. These include software to run library management systems, document publishing and distribution software, document delivery systems, search engines, telecommunications networks and their services, computer hardware, training programmes and a host of other professional services (such as cleaning, accountancy and marketing) which contribute to the operation of the organizations in the information industry. Some of these might be regarded as information products in their own right.

| Goods and documents (most exist in both print and electronic formats) | |
| --- | --- |
| Periodicals | Learned journals/academic journals |
| | Professional journals |
| | Magazines |
| | Newspapers |
| | Newsletters and bulletin boards |
| Reference documents | Encyclopedias |
| | Dictionaries |
| | Bibliographies and bibliographic databases |
| | Directories and databanks |
| Books | Adult fiction, classics |
| | Adult fiction, popular |
| | Adult non-fiction, learned, textbooks |
| | Adult non-fiction, popular |
| | Children's fiction |
| | Children's non-fiction |
| | Paperback books |
| | Hardcover books |
| Others | Published reports from government and other agencies |
| | Videos |
| | Music CDs |
| | DVD |
| | Multimedia documents |
| | Government publications |
| | Corporate reports – technical and business |
| | Patents |
| | Conference proceedings |

**Services**
Information services
Document delivery and interlibrary loans services
End-user training
Market research agencies
Information service providers (ISPs)
Current awareness services
Help desk services
Consultancy services
Financial and business information services
Entertainment services
Computing services

**Figure 2.1**   Some end-user product categories

# CUSTOMERS

Customers are the other party in the marketing exchange. Who are the customers in the information marketplace? Everybody uses information, either to support their business and professional activities or for education, leisure or community involvement, so that every member of a population is a potential customer for some type of information product or service. To be converted into an actual customer, they need to make a purchase, make use of a library and information service, or access a database. The first of these applies to a relatively restricted range of information products that are available in the information marketplace. In many other instances, information and documents are accessed through an intermediary, such as a library, an information broker, or some other corporate purchasing arrangement. Users of information exhibit reluctance to pay for something as ephemeral as information (unless it is packaged as a product, such as a book, a video or a CD), and it is therefore often the case that the user of the information is not the purchaser. Purchasers are typically information intermediaries, such as library and information services, or knowledge centres.

The concept of the customer is explored more fully in Chapter 3, which deals with the interpretation of the customer concept in a public service context, and the distinctions between organizational and consumer markets and their customers. Figure 2.2 offers a simple perspective on the different terms used for customer in various contexts, and emphasizes the all-embracing nature of the term 'customer' which, whilst useful in discussing concepts such as marketing orientation, needs to be interpreted according to context.

Figure 2.3 lists some categories of customers, which might be helpful in thinking about the nature of the customer in this context. It is important to emphasize, however, that in order to respond effectively to the needs of groups of customers, organizations must segment their customers into groups of people with similar needs, and then create a profile of that group.

Customers may have a number of different contract arrangements with an information provider, for example:

- purchase, in which the buyer acquires the right to use the item thenceforth, including, should they so choose, sharing it with others;

| Context | 'Customer' term |
|---------|-----------------|
| Public library | Readers, borrowers |
| Academic library | Users, readers, learners |
| Bookshop | Buyers |
| Website | Surfers, visitors |
| Newspaper | Readers |
| Workplace library | Clients |
| Professional body information service | Members |
| Journal | Subscribers |

**Figure 2.2** Some terms for customer

| General public, e.g. | Adults |
| --- | --- |
| | Children |
| | Special groups, e.g. the housebound, the blind |
| Professional groups, e.g. | Dentists |
| | Hospital doctors |
| | Accountants |
| | Lawyers |
| Academic users, e.g. | Children |
| | Adults – students |
| | Adults – staff |
| Business users, e.g. | Research and development scientists |
| | Marketers |
| | Managers |
| | Administrators |
| Information intermediaries, e.g. | Knowledge agents within organizations |
| | Information brokers and consultants |

**Figure 2.3**   Some categories of information customers

- borrowing, in which the user has rights of use for a limited period of time. Borrowing is thus a way of rationing and sharing scarce resources (normally in a public service context); and
- licence, in which terms of use are specified. The right to use usually terminates at the end of the contract period.

The nature of such contracts will affect customer behaviour and issues associated with building relationships with customers, which are explored in Chapters 3 and 4.

Organizations are also customers in the information marketplace. Every organization in the supply chain from the producers of intellectual content to redistributors and users are both suppliers and customers.

## PROFILING THE INFORMATION INDUSTRY

Figure 2.4 lists some of the key stakeholders in the traditional publishing process and describes their roles in terms that are applicable in both a print-based and an electronic environment. The environment influences both the way in which the product is created, as in, for example, electronic refereeing or editing, and the nature of the final product, as in for example, a multimedia encyclopedia. In some contexts some of these roles may be merged, or one organization may adopt more than one role. Many of the stakeholder categories can be split into other sub-categories: thus in the redistributor's role we might also include national document delivery centres, cooperative interlibrary loan services, com-

19

| Role | Example |
| --- | --- |
| Producers of intellectual content | Authors, illustrators, multimedia creation teams |
| Controllers of intellectual content, with reference to quality standards and suitability | Editors, referees, reviewers |
| Publishers establish a corporate brand image and acts as an interface between producers of intellectual content and distributor | Publishers, printers, database producers |
| Distributors ensure that the document/ information reaches the potential customers and engages in appropriate promotion | Library supply agents, booksellers, Websites, online hosts, Videotex services, Audiotex services, distributors of CD-ROM |
| Archivers maintain archival copy for later retrieval | Libraries, private collectors |
| Redistributors make documents or information available to others | Libraries, educational institutions through copying for students, information consultants |
| Users | Corporate and individual users |

**Figure 2.4**   Stakeholder roles in the electronic information marketplace

mercial document delivery services, offprints and reprints, and current-awareness service suppliers. Each category of stakeholders hides a whole sector of organizations that will be concerned to stay in business and to develop their existing competencies, product and service range, and customer base to secure a position in the developing marketplace. There is already some competition for the roles of publisher and distributor from organizations such as Microsoft and some of the telecommunication service providers.

A microcosm of how different stakeholders operate in the information market-place can be seen in the channels through which documents are delivered. The ability to deliver any document in response to a demand and at speed requires significant document collections, coupled with access routes to other document depositories. The issues differ according to types of documents, with a very clear division between the two major categories: books and journal articles. Books are normally lent or purchased, whereas journal articles are often delivered as copies for retention in the form of photocopies, electronic copy or fax. Over the years libraries have worked together in consortia and networks to support one another in meeting demand for documents that are not held by the library that receives the request. In addition, publishers, as distributors, need to strike a balance between maintaining relationships with their libraries as customers and maximizing sales of books and periodicals to end-users. Other agencies in the supply chain, such as library suppliers and booksellers, also have businesses to protect.

Figure 2.5 shows a range of different options for document delivery channels. These may be categorized on the basis of the agents involved, or on the basis of other criteria, including:

Publisher → User
Publisher → Library supplier → Library → User
Publisher → Database producer → Document delivery service → User
Publisher → Bookseller → User
Publisher → Library → User
Publisher → Online search service → User
User → User
Organization → User
Organization → Organization

**Figure 2.5** **Some modes of document delivery**

- whether the document is delivered directly to the end-user at their desk top or to the library as intermediary;
- the format of the document. The issues are different for books, journals, journal articles and reference works such as directories;
- the media in or through which the document is distributed. This might include CD-ROM, fax, or online/Web;
- the nature of the delivery contract.

*REFLECT: Give examples of the modes of document delivery proposed in Figure 2.5.*

The presentation in Figure 2.4, in focusing on roles, does not draw out another important feature of the information marketplace: the diversity of the objectives and funding bases of the players in this marketplace. For each different group of players, a number of organizations are either in competitive or collaborative relationships with one another. Many organizations fulfil a number of the roles in Figure 2.4 through different products or services in their portfolio, and may therefore have relationships across different product areas in the information marketplace. An important feature of the information marketplace is that it embraces both commercial organizations such as publishers and public sector organizations such as public libraries. For example, organizations might design a Web portal to support their users in locating useful information, but their motives for doing so might be quite different. In creating such a portal, publishers, probably in collaboration with a bookseller, will be seeking to encourage consumers to make a purchase. A public library will be seeking to fulfil its function as a public service, and to offer guidance to members of a community on useful and evaluated sources of information. Large organizations also have sizeable publishing operations, often now embedded in their knowledge management initiatives. They might design a portal on their intranet so that employees can have access to the information they need to support research and development, market research or decision-making. The word 'web' is an appropriate term to use to describe a network of resources with hyperlinks between them. It would be an equally appropriate description of the relationships in the information marketplace.

## COMPETITORS, PARTNERS AND CONSORTIA

Early economic theory viewed different businesses as being in a competitive marketplace, in which all businesses were in competition with each other for customer attention and transactions. As is explored more fully in Chapter 10, a more sophisticated view recognizes that for continued business success, organizations need to differentiate themselves from one another by offering products and services which are either different, or perceived by customers as such. Through this process of differentiation, each organization seeks to fill a unique niche or role in the marketplace. Organizations may differentiate themselves on the basis of their product portfolio, brand portfolio, price range, promotional activities (such as audience and marketing message), service (including the features and quality of service), and place or mode of delivery (such as print or electronic). Key assets in maintaining successful differentiation are the competencies of the company, which reside in its people, its processes, its physical assets and its knowledge base, together with its capacity to respond to competitive challenges. Successful businesses are aware of their assets, their strengths and their weaknesses, and are able continually to develop their strengths in order to ensure that they continue to be relevant and adequate.

When an organization recognizes that it requires additional competence, perhaps in terms of technology or familiarity with a different marketplace, one solution is to enter into a partnership, strategic alliance (including merger or acquisition) or joint venture. The success of such an initiative depends on the expectation and achievement of mutual benefits, and on shared objectives and culture. In other words, successful organizations work proactively with others to deliver a solution to the marketplace.

*REFLECT: Identify the organization that you regard as your most significant competitor. How would you convert them to a partner?*

The information world abounds in collaborative ventures, embracing both the public and private sectors. Driven by a commitment to public good, the academic and public library community worldwide set up the early library cooperatives, now library consortia. Libraries have formed library cooperatives and networks for many decades. Such networks have played a major role in resource-sharing and in the development of computerized library management systems. Networks in Europe and the United States, such as BLCMP, LASER, OCLC and WLIN, have now been well established since the late 1960s. Many of these library network ventures were early participants in the exploitation of computerization and have been major proponents of the development and implementation of library management systems. Library cooperatives have made significant contributions to the realization of the electronic library, through the continuing evolution of library management systems and the creation of large shared bibliographic databases that have significantly reduced original cataloguing. Currently such networks are serving as focal points for developments associated with electronic document delivery, electronic journals and a variety of Web-based facilities that provide access to a wide range of other databases and information resources.

In the past few years, a range of UK and EU government and government agency initiatives associated with creating a knowledge-based society and economy, covering themes such as lifelong learning, the global marketplace, ICT for all, and social inclusion, have encouraged collaboration within the public sector, and between the public and commercial sectors. Figure 2.6 lists some examples of collaborative ventures. They represent a very much larger number of projects, but have been selected to demonstrate the range and diversity of collaboration in the information industry. Collaboration is not restricted to initiatives driven by the public sector, but is common to many organizations in the information industry. Perhaps indicative of this climate is the following extract from a recent job advertisement for a post in the public library sector:

> the post holder will help to drive the development of the service by building effective partnerships with bodies inside and outside the organization, and will be responsible for bids for grant funding from appropriate sources.

*REFLECT: Examine the Website of your local public library. How many organizations are identified on this Website as partners of the public library?*

## CHARACTERISTICS AND CONSTRAINTS

There are a number of issues that characterize the information marketplace, and a range of constraints on its continued development. Some of these have been implicit in the earlier discussion in this chapter; here they are stated more explicitly.

### Changing technology

Currently, information, information systems and associated communications are gradually increasing their impact on society and its values. The ultimate scenario

23

| Name and aim of project | Collaborators | Funding sources and sponsors |
|---|---|---|
| Youthboox<br>*Aim*: to link the relationship-building skills of youth workers with those of librarians | National Youth Agency, Wellworth Reading (run by the county libraries of Dorset, Hampshire, and West Sussex) | Arts Council of England |
| Paperback originals<br>*Aim*: to make it possible for public libraries to stock the latest books at the same time as they reach the shops | Branching Out (a group of public libraries), Flamingo Books (HarperCollins) | Books for Students |
| Voyage into books<br>*Aim*: to link writers and artists with socially excluded kids | West Sussex Library Service | Arts Council of England |
| Tomorrow's history<br>*Aim*: to set up an online database that will link communities to their heritage | Information North (a North East England libraries consortium) | Millennium Festival Fund |
| Web of Science<br>*Aim*: access to Web interface providing access to citation databases from the Institute for Scientific Information (ISI) | ISI, Joint Information Systems Committee (JISC), Combined Higher Education Software Team (CHEST), Manchester Information and Associated Services (MIMAS) | Various |
| Comfort+plus carpets<br>*Aim*: to provide tailored carpets for library and other public spaces | Reska Products Ltd, Milliken Carpets | |
| Library Association's (LA) Workplace libraries '99 campaign<br>*Aim*: to realize and release the power of information | Library Association | Anbar, Blackwells, Bloomsbury and others |
| Resource Discovery Network Centre<br>*Aim*: to identify and describe high quality Internet resources and broker access to widely distributed electronic services and resources | Kings College London, University of Bath | JISC |
| INTER-ALL<br>*Aim*: to bring the advantage of information technology, the Internet, video conferencing and business information to small to medium-sized businesses in the region. | The Library Partnership West Midlands | |

**Figure 2.6**  Some examples of collaborative projects

of the virtual society, where all communication is electronic, and processes such as teleworking, e-learning and videoconferencing substitute for actual person-to-person contact, has significant implications for the way in which human beings satisfy their need for interaction with each another. This makes the information marketplace particularly challenging and unpredictable. More specifically, change is associated with:

- computer technologies upon which applications are based;
- the way in which communities communicate and learn.

Major efforts in recent years have been associated with the development of more user-friendly interfaces that are more suitable for the consumer marketplace and networking. Both of these developments have contributed to the increasing penetration of the Internet and the Web.

Increasing penetration into home markets will affect both consumer markets for information products and the marketing communication channels available to providers. Relatively new technologies, such as digital television and mobile technologies delivered through a mobile phone, will affect the range of potential future products. Certainly, convergence of technologies in the computer, television and telecommunications industry is well under way, and is triggering global mergers and strategic alliances across all sectors of the information industry.

## Globalization

Communities and businesses are increasingly functioning in a global society and marketplace. E-commerce through global networks, such as the Web, is further fuelling globalization. The information marketplace has always been global. Publishers, database providers and online search services have long since ceased to operate within national boundaries, and even public sector organizations such as the British Library have a worldwide customer base. However, some participants, such as public libraries, are established to serve specific communities, usually within one geographical district. This approach to providing access to knowledge is not consistent with the fact that improved telecommunications allow people to gather information irrespective of geographical location (although language continues to present a barrier). In a global marketplace, information and knowledge providers are open to global competition, and, in addition need to take a global perspective to production and delivery. Currency fluctuations may present serious threats to business stability. Further, certain types of information and knowledge will be available to global audiences; this information will not provide organizations or states with competitive advantage, but will be a necessary platform on which to build further knowledge that may, in turn, differentiate them in the marketplace.

## The network enterprise

The nature of corporations is undergoing change. Global corporate strategic alliances have had a significant impact on marketplaces, employment and national economies. Information technology has increased organizational capacity to form business networks and networked enterprises. This will affect the customer base of specific information producers.

## Knowledge-based economies

As governments recognize the significance of their knowledge assets, both explicitly in formal knowledge repositories and implicitly in the skills and abilities of their citizens, they will need to intervene in the information marketplace to ensure that appropriate information is available to support education, learning and training, and other aspects of capitalizing on the value of knowledge assets. As the value of information becomes more widely recognized, and access is made more straightforward, the gap between those who have access to information and those who do not will widen, and sections of society will be exposed to even higher levels of exclusion. Such groups may be served by community libraries, neighbourhood resource centres and public networks. In order that citizens can capitalize on the information available to them, governments must support life-long learning and the development of skills in the use of ICT and information.

## Intellectual property and copyright issues

Quality information, whether it be text, statistics or multimedia, costs time, effort and money to create. Producers seek to recoup their investment. Yet, with advances in technology and the advent of electronic documents, it is difficult to enforce appropriate copyright protection. It is too easy to copy or download sections of databases.

## Security, data protection and privacy

Some data, including, for example, financial transactions, national security and commercially sensitive data need to be protected. As organizations are increasingly opening up extranets that give customers and partners access to sections of their corporate data, the issue of security for these organizations becomes more pressing. Within organizations, knowledge management initiatives require that organizations formulate a clear view of what knowledge is made available to which audiences. Adequate security measures are necessary to protect knowledge from those who should not be able to access it.

In addition, data protection is necessary to safeguard the privacy of the individual. Commercial organizations already have the capacity to build databases that extend beyond mailing-list details such as name and address to complete profiles of purchasing habits. Loyalty cards in supermarkets and library registration cards generate data that can be used to profile the behaviour and interests of individuals. E-commerce applications can generate complete profiles of the searching and e-purchasing behaviours of individuals. Tutors who need to investigate potential cases of plagiarism can check which sites a student has visited. Organizations can check whether employees are visiting legitimate sites that contribute to their job, and credit card details supplied as part of a purchase transaction have the potential to provide unwarranted access to personal financial information. Data protection legislation intervenes in such situations and ensures the acceptable use of personal information.

## Standards

Competitive advantage can be achieved by a significant business in the software or technology area of the information marketplace if it can make its standards for a new technology the *de facto* standard for the industry. On the other hand, adherence to standards is an essential feature for all participants in a networked information community. Successful mechanisms for establishing standards are essential. Standards bodies have a role to play, but it is also the case that the market/power struggle in relation to standards is likely to recur with each new advance in technology.

## Archiving and bibliographical control

One of the cultural functions of art galleries, museums and libraries is the maintenance of an archival record of cultural assets, including documents and other representative items. The maintenance and storage of such archives in a form that makes them accessible to scholars and the general public is an expensive enterprise. Many of the individual items in such archives may only be accessed infrequently, if at all, and it may be difficult to justify their retention on the basis of use. Libraries house significant collections of print documents, some of which can be archived in electronic or microfilm format. Conversion to electronic format may make rare documents and special collections more easily accessible to a global audience, but it does not always eliminate the need to retain and preserve the original. Special collections of documents, manuscripts and other items, sometimes associated with famous literary, political or scientific figures, may be extremely valuable on the open marketplace; such collections represent hidden assets that may form the basis of a unique service with a global audience.

Electronic documents pose many problems for the maintenance of an archival record. Such documents may be dynamic and changing, and the creation of a number of different versions is relatively easy. Information on the Web is notoriously volatile. Which version should form the archive document? Clearly it is difficult to decide what constitutes a document; it is also difficult to maintain bibliographical control over these documents. Other problems include:

- what data should be archived?
- which storage media should be used?
- how long will the database last without deterioration?
- how can individuals access archived databases?

## THE MARKETING ENVIRONMENT

The wider context in which the information marketplace functions, referred to as its marketing environment, has an important influence on the way in which customer needs evolve and the options available to the organization to meet those needs. In other words, the marketing environment affects all aspects of marketing, from product to price and promotion to the strength of relationships in the supply chain, and other collaborative arrangements. The marketing environment is shaped by a wide variety of factors and influences; these are normally grouped under the four headings: sociocultural; technological; economic and competitive; and political and legal influences. These influences (see Figure 2.7) are represented by the acronym STEP. Although each of these factors will be discussed separately below, there is considerable interdependence between them. So, for example, licensing regulations that are formulated between major CD-ROM suppliers and library consortia are influenced by the options offered by technology in terms of downloading information, and the societal need for access to knowledge in support of learning. Examples of these influences are presented in Figure 2.8.

### SOCIOCULTURAL INFLUENCES

Sociocultural influences include both quantitative data such as demographic trends and data about less tangible concepts such as tastes, attitudes and cultures. Demographic trends profile a population in terms of age, sex, income,

| Sociocultural | Technological |
|---|---|
| • Demographic<br>• Culture<br>• Attitudes<br>• Current issues | Innovation affecting<br>• Products<br>• Materials/components<br>• Processes<br>• Distribution<br>• Marketing/administration |
| **Economic/competitive** | **Political/legal** |
| • Market structure<br>• Government policy<br>• Trading blocs<br>• Taxation<br>• Interest rates | • The EU<br>• National government<br>• Local government<br>• Regulatory bodies<br>• Trade associations |

*Source:* based on Brassington and Pettitt (1997), p. 39

**Figure 2.7** Influences in the marketing environment

**Sociocultural**
Age distribution of target market
Changes in social status and wealth of society
Changes in educational levels
Changes in ethnic and racial mix
**Technological**
Telecommunications standards and protocols
New software products, such as improved search-engine technology
Telecommunication networks with enhanced bandwidth
Optical storage media
Portable storage media with enhanced capacity
Enhanced multimedia document creation, publishing and management software
**Economic/competitive**
Prices of journals
Prices of books
Entry of other information providers with different roles
Prices of electronic information
**Political/legal**
Central and local funding decisions for public and national libraries
Funding decisions for higher education
Increases in student numbers in further and higher education
Copyright legislation
Licensing agreements in respect of the use of data downloaded from databases
Governmental and institutional controls that suggest that library services should be provided 'free' to the customer

**Figure 2.8** Some examples of environmental influences on the information marketplace

family size and household structure. Whilst these data can be useful in, for example, gauging how many over 55s there will be in the population in two years' time, and therefore in identifying how many people might be potential customers for an 'Introducing the Web' course for this group, attitudes may be much more important in determining the actual take-up. The information marketer may also need to be sensitive to the concerns of consumer and pressure groups in areas such as environmental issues, animal welfare, personal health and corporate and personal ethics.

*REFLECT: What effect is average family size of a population likely to have on the percentage of 18–23-year-olds in full-time higher education?*

## TECHNOLOGICAL INFLUENCES

Technology has already been discussed at some length in the context of the information marketplace, and has been recognized as a major driver for change. Specifically, technology may affect organizations at a number of different levels:

- advances in materials, components and products, such as are evident in the hardware platforms which underlie the information industry;
- production processes, with word processing and document creation software (encompassing multimedia capabilities) having changed the way in which information products are created. A good example of technological innovation in the service sector is the effect of satellite technology, computerized exchanges and fibre-optic cable, which have reduced costs and increased access and speed of communication for customers;
- administration and distribution, often in support of enhanced customer service, and reductions in lead times between ordering and delivery EDI in the book trade has reduced the time between order and delivery of books, and therefore the speed with which libraries can make books available to users. The record-keeping associated with such ordering has also been streamlined with the aid of technology;
- marketing and customers. Technology has provided new means of communicating with customers through the Internet, including Websites, and two-way communication through e-mail and interactive Websites. Databases have facilitated more targeted marketing, which will increasingly fuel the personalization of the relationship between the organization and its customers.

## ECONOMIC/COMPETITIVE INFLUENCES

The economic/competitive environment can be considered at two levels: macroeconomic and microeconomic. The former environment is the backdrop that determines fundamental parameters that affect all organizations. Factors include taxation, government spending and interest rates, and the operation and influences of trading blocs, such as the EU and EFTA.

The microeconomic environment is concerned with the structure of the individual marketplace. The most accurate description of the information marketplace is that it is in a state of monopolistic competition. This term refers to an economic model in which many competitors are in the market, but each has a product that is sufficiently differentiated from the rest to create a kind of monopoly for itself, because there is no direct substitute. However, like any marketing situation, this state may be subject to change and challenge.

## POLITICAL/LEGAL INFLUENCES

Political and legal influences include laws, regulations and codes of practice from national governments, the EU, local government, statutory bodies and trade associations. National governments have in recent years been responsible for the privatization and/or marketization of significant industries that were previously operated as state-owned monopolies. Regulations relating to marketing communications vary widely between countries and significant work is being undertaken within the EU to change this situation. Within the UK, the Advertising Standards Authority (ASA) administers the British Code of Advertising Practice and the British Code of Sales Promotion Practice.

*REFLECT: Visit the Website of the Advertising Standards Authority, and review the information that it provides on its activities.*

Aspects of all the STEP influences are subject to continual change; the marketing environment is dynamic, and it is important that organizations are aware of these changes. In order to achieve this, organizations, and individuals on their behalf, need to engage in **environmental scanning**. This is the collection and evaluation of information from the marketing environment that might affect the organization and its strategic marketing activities. Such information may be embedded in a number of different types of sources, including personal contacts, experience, published market research reports, marketing information systems, government statistics, trade associations, the trade and professional press and commissioned market research. Extracts from such sources should be gathered to form the knowledge base of the organization, and made accessible to those involved with organizational and marketing decision-making. The issues of information sources and the management of environmental scanning are explored more fully in Chapter 9 on collecting marketing information.

## CONCLUSION

The information marketplace has many unique features that derive from the nature of information products, coupled with the wider role of information in the social, cultural and business life of a community. Although the competitive structure of the information marketplace can be described as that of monopolistic competition in which most players have identified a unique role and niche, these niches are continually under threat. Relationships between organizations are complex and multi-faceted. Collaborative and cooperative alliances and consortia feature significantly. Whilst technology is a major force for change, other STEP factors also contribute to the dynamic nature of the information marketplace.

## REFERENCES AND FURTHER READING

Arnold, S.E. (1990), 'Marketing electronic information: theory, practice and challenges 1980–1990', in *Annual Review of Information Science and Technology*, 25 ed. M.E. Williams, Amsterdam and Oxford: ASIS, pp. 87–144.

Blunden, B. and Blunden, M. (eds) (1994), *The Electronic Publishing Business and its Market*, Leatherhead: IEPRC/Pira International.

Boulding, K. (1968), 'Knowledge as a commodity', in *Beyond Economics: Essays on Society, Religion and Ethics*. Ann Arbor, Michigan: University of Michigan Press.

Brassington, F. and Pettitt, S. (1997), *Principles of Marketing*. London: Pitman Publishing.

Brindley, L.J. (1993), 'Information service and information product pricing', *Aslib Proceedings*, **45** (11/12), November/December, 297–305.

Coote, H. and Batchelor, B. (1998), *How to Market your Library Service Effectively*. 2nd edition. London: Aslib. (Aslib Know How Series, ed. S.P. Webb.)

Cronin, B. and Gudim, M. (1986), 'Information and productivity: A review of research', *International Journal of Information Management*, **6**(2), 85–101.

De Saez, E.E. (1997), *Marketing Concepts for Libraries and Information Services*. London: Library Association.

Eaton, J.J. and Bawden, D. (1991), 'What kind of resource is information?', *International Journal of Information Management*, **11**, 156–65.

Hart, K. (1999), *Putting Marketing Ideas into Action*. London: Library Association. (The Successful LIS Professional Series, ed. S. Pantry.)

Schwuchow, W. (1995), 'Measuring the "information market(s)": a personal experience', *Journal of Information Science*, **21**(2), 123–32.

# 3 Customers

## AIMS

This chapter reviews a range of concepts associated with the customer, organizational markets and consumer buying behaviour. An understanding of customers and the benefits they seek from an organization is central to the marketing concept and a marketing orientation. The following topics are explored in this chapter:

- the distinction between organizational and consumer markets;
- the customer concept in the public sector;
- customers, benefits and segmentation;
- the consumer decision-making process; and
- consumer behaviour.

## INTRODUCTION

Earlier chapters of this book have emphasized the centrality of the customer to marketing and marketing orientation within any organization. This chapter, then, focuses on customers and an organization's relationship with them. What do we know about our customers? Have we thought about what makes them use an information product or service in the first place, and later, what factors ensure customer retention or return? Do library managers think not just in terms of which services customers use, but more fundamentally in terms of the benefits that customers seek from an information service? With a view to encouraging a fresh perspective on some of these issues, this chapter examines some of the key concepts concerned with customers and consumer buying behaviour. We start with a review of the differences between two key types of markets: consumer and organizational. An understanding of the nature of customers in the public sector is important for many information services. The concepts associated with customers, such as consumer buying behaviour, loyalty, retention and segmentation, often have their roots in commercial organizations. Nevertheless, these concepts provide a useful framework for analysing customer groups and considering responses and offerings to those groups. Customers, or, more specifically, consumers, seek benefits. In order to offer an effective product portfolio or service we must identify customer segments, taking into account the benefits that customers seek. Yet this is not sufficient. It is also important to acknowledge that the consumer decision-making process influences purchasing and use of services. Some key concepts in this area are introduced.

## ORGANIZATIONAL AND CONSUMER MARKETS

Dibb et al. (1994) define consumer markets and organizational markets thus:

> Consumer markets are comprised of individuals who consume for benefit from the purchased product, and do not buy the product with the main purpose of making a profit. Organizational markets consist of individuals or groups who buy for one of three purposes: resale, direct use in producing other products, or use in general daily operations.

It is generally recognized that there are significant differences between organizational markets and consumer markets. Any business that is confronted with operating in both types of marketplaces (and this includes many information providers) needs to appreciate these differences, and the consequences for marketing management. Consumer and organizational markets can be compared in terms of the following characteristics, based on Bernard (1995), and Kotler (1994).

- **Customers** – organizational markets are characterized by a smaller number of customers than usually exist in consumer markets. This typically results in a smaller number of transactions, but these are likely to be of higher aggregate value. Customers, although scattered, may be relatively easily identifiable. In consumer markets the potential customer base may be large, it may be difficult to identify customers, and customers are frequently geographically scattered.
- **Demand** for organizational customers is derived from various stages in the distribution chain. Consumer demand tends to be triggered more directly.
- **Technical complexity** of product being offered is often greater in organizational markets that are highly specialized in their requirements. Marketers need familiarity with product specification and functionality. Whilst this may be less necessary in consumer markets, with complex information-based

products the need for user-friendly features and help lines starts to mirror the support required in organizational markets.

- **Buying processes are more complex** in organizational markets than in consumer markets, as discussed below. Organizational buyers are likely to be able to exercise expertise in their assessment of the product offering.
- **Marketing communication** – personal selling and other targeted methods of communication, such as direct marketing and database marketing, are prevalent in organizational markets. There is some focus on the development of relationships between organizations, sometimes to the extent that personalized products are created for the buyer, and product development may be a collaborative venture. Marketing communications in consumer markets embraces mass media, such as television and billboards, but for most information products it involves communication with targeted groups.
- **Price** – in organizational markets the pricing strategy is central to defining and maintaining the relationship between the buyer and the seller. Negotiation, contract arrangements and discounts are common. Most consumer markets expect pricing to be one-off for goods, and on a subscription or payment-for-use basis for services.
- **Competitors** – organizational markets comprise a limited number of competitors, each with carefully honed technical expertise, reputations, market positions and relationships, and there are benefits to be derived from mutual support between buyer and supplier. Consumer markets that are subject to rapid technological change and have low entry barriers, as is the case for many information products, are likely to witness a relatively high level of new products, and competition may be severe.

Rowley (1998) uses the case of the online search services to illustrate the changes to marketing mix that were necessary to make the transition from a largely organizational market to an end-consumer market. Initially, online search services were mostly used by information intermediaries, and purchase transactions were effectively those of an organizational marketplace. It remains the case that many of these services are still purchased through organizational buying processes, but the services have been remodelled to affect both direct sales to end-consumers and user and influencer impact in organizational buying processes.

## CUSTOMERS AND THE PUBLIC SECTOR

In addition to the differentiation between organizations and consumers as customers, a significant issue in many information environments is the public sector context in which information provision is managed. Information provision has been seen, and will continue to be seen, as a significant political agenda, because it has far-reaching implications for the economic and social welfare of countries and states. Accordingly, in a public sector context there are often a number of interested parties, in addition to the user of the information, who may have an interest, or represent the interests of others or society in general, in information provision. This requires a more sophisticated perspective on the nature of a customer.

The **societal marketing concept** recognizes organizations' ethical and social responsibility as part of a global community and challenges businesses and specifically marketers to address the potential conflict between consumer wants, consumer interests and long-run societal welfare in their marketing policies and strategies.

Whilst the societal marketing concept might provide a perspective on marketing that is more palatable for public sector services, it is important to acknowledge the polarization of attitudes towards marketing in the public sector in general, and libraries specifically, typified by:

- a recognition of the importance of establishing an appropriate relationship with the customer, as is evidenced, for example, in pubic libraries through an emphasis on customer care and in academic libraries through the appointment of subject specialists or academic link librarians;
- an aversion to the dedication of funds to any but the most modest of promotional efforts. Certainly, the marketing manager remains an elusive character in libraries, and the public sector in general.

There is a wide range of stakeholder groups, including local government officers, the electorate, local and national businesses, political parties and pressure groups, in addition to the end-consumer, their families and friends. This diversity of stakeholders provokes questions about who is the customer, or who represents the customer in a specific marketing context. The different groups of stakeholders in the public sector each have a different experience of the public sector service. These stakeholders all have different roles in service definition, the evaluation of service quality and participation in the service experience. For example, in education, although all stakeholders are concerned with the 'end-product', they are concerned to varying extents with the process associated with the creation of the product. Employers and society in general are concerned primarily with the 'product' of the system, whereas students and arguably their families will also be concerned with the process.

In addition many public services are engaged in offering services to other public services. For example, academic libraries offer services to students and staff. In the case of students, libraries offer a component of the total service experience that a student undergoes in a further or higher education institution. Academic staff have a different relationship with the library from that enjoyed by students. Whilst they are in some senses customers in their own right, the quality of the information service that they receive will indirectly affect their delivery to the students. Their experience will affect both the knowledge that they impart to students, and also, because the efficient delivery of library services will affect their work patterns and loading, the time that they have to devote to them. The provision of a service to such customers and the quality of relationships with them are, then, often central to efficient and effective operations within the organization, and hence to customer service delivered by other parts of the organization.

Another useful distinction is that between citizen, customer and consumer:

- **Citizens** generally have rights of access to public services, and may be vociferous through political channels and pressure groups in ensuring that appropriate services are available. Thus citizens' rights might include access to education for children between 4 and 18, and access to hospitals when needed. Most citizens do not exercise these rights most of the time, but they still expect the service to be available to them when they need it.
- **Customers** is the generic term for any stakeholders, individuals or groups for whom the organization in some way provides a good or service.
- **Consumers** are the users of the service.

There is clearly an overlap between these groups, and members of one group will influence the attitudes and behaviours of members of other groups through word of mouth across family and social networks. Consumers for public sector organizations are generally a subset of customers. Most customers are citizens, but, due to geographical boundaries and other factors, they may not always have right of access to the public services over which they have some influence. The issue of customer roles is explored more fully below in the context of consumer behaviour.

*REFLECT: List the stakeholders for a public sector service with which you are associated. If possible give their role and job title, and their name.*

## CUSTOMERS, BENEFITS AND SEGMENTATION

Customers seek **benefits** or **solutions**, not products. When they buy a product, whether a good or a service, they buy a cluster of product features, but may only want one or two of these. Generally customers are seen as members of a market. A **market** is an aggregate of people who, as individuals or in organizations, have needs for products in a product class and the ability, willingness and authority to purchase such products.

Normally undifferentiated marketing is unsuccessful, and some kind of **segmentation** is introduced as an aid to profiling customers and gaining a better understanding of them and the benefits they seek. All members of a **market segment** have some relevant characteristics in common. Segmentation offers:

- a better understanding of customers and their needs;
- a better understanding of competitors;
- more effective targeting of resources, and tailored marketing communication to specific target markets.

Market segments are defined in terms of a set of criteria, and the choice of appropriate criteria is critical to the design of an appropriate marketing offering. There is a range of segmentation variables, or ways to segment markets. Demographic variables such as geography and location, age, sex, occupation and social class have traditionally been used for market segmentation. These have been popular, not because they are necessarily the best segmentation variables, but rather because the data on these variables are relatively readily available. Good segmentation relates to customer needs, and should be informed by the factors that influence the consumer purchasing process as summarized at the end of this chapter in Figure 3.9 (pp. 50–51).

Marketers have explored psychographic or lifestyle segmentation, which seeks to segment consumers not only on demographic characteristics, but also on attitudes to life, beliefs and aspirations, activities and interests. Database marketing has pushed the precision of market analysis further, and is moving in the direction of treating each consumer as an individual target. One recent development that might make it easier to profile customers on this basis is intelligent agents that, for example, create a profile of a customer's purchasing preferences on the basis of their previous choices and searches in an e-shopping environment. Intelligent agents can also create similar profiles of individuals' information interests, and thereby support their search for information on the Web. Information products are often delivered interactively to consumers, and consumers are sometimes prepared to participate in the personalization of these products. Search tools and other aids assist personalization. There is a significant group of information products for which the most appropriate market segmentation is micro segmentation, in which customers are treated as individuals.

Behaviour segmentation seeks to focus on the individual's relationship with the product. Factors such as end-use, benefits sought, usage rate, loyalty, attitude and buyer readiness may be taken into account.

Market segments must be:

- measurable and identifiable, so that they can be characterized (in terms of segmentation variables such as age or profession); the best situation is when members of the segment can be listed, and the size of the segment is known;
- sufficiently large to justify expenditure associated with service and product delivery, promotional activities and, in commercial contexts, to ensure a profit. However, not all segments need be large; sometimes, small segments can have a significant effect on profit or on influencing funding decisions;
- accessible, with an appropriate marketing mix and, in particular, there must be channels of communication, such as newsletters, mailing lists and television channels which support targeted communication with this group. This criterion tends to constrain organizations to work within segments already identified by editors, producers and others involved with communications;
- relevant to the type of market. For example, segmentation on the basis of pets owned is relevant in the pet food market but not in the car market.

Figure 3.1 shows some characteristics that may be used for segmentation of information users.

*REFLECT: Are the characteristics listed in Figure 3.1 likely to generate segments that reflect the benefits sought by customers?*

The conventional focus for segmentation activities is on the user or the customer. Some public sector services may be required to ensure that any segmentation

1. Age – public libraries often segment into early readers, teenagers and adults, and recognize the need to offer different services for these groups, and to communicate with appropriate language and imagery.
2. Location – often relates to the physical location of service provider with respect to the home or office location of the potential user. For public libraries, the issue of distance may be significant, whereas for a workplace library a global user community may mean that the service and marketing communications are delivered over networks.
3. Frequency of use – loyalty benefits may be available for regular customers, or inducements might be helpful for non-users or infrequent users or customers.
4. Day and/or time of use – service access, such as opening times, may need to accommodate times when users are available to use the service.
5. Ability or willingness to pay – may be an important factor in services where there is a charge to the end-consumer.
6. Job function or status – in a workplace library, different marketing incentives might be appropriate for staff, depending upon their job role.
7. Subject interest.
8. Preferred information delivery mechanism – personal contact, telephone, fax, or e-mail.
9. Purpose of information use – options include leisure, education, businesses, professional and research.

**Figure 3.1** Some characteristics for segmenting users of information services

is wider than this, and includes all citizens. The purpose of segmentation, and the link between segmentation for service or product design and for marketing communications, may affect whether segmentation is determined by the user base, or the potential user base. One group should not be overlooked in any segmentation exercise – the array of stakeholders who may affect funding or business opportunities. If these stakeholders are non-users, the segmentation of such customers is not relevant to service delivery, but its purpose is to inform the design of marketing messages addressed to this group. Many of these messages will be embedded in management information and reports on suc-cesses and progress. All management information conveys a marketing message!

Segmentation is also applicable in organizational markets, and fulfils a similar function of allowing the supplying organization to profile its customers. However, the number of organizations that form the customer base of any one organization can vary considerably. Some organizations work with only one or a few other organizations, and will therefore treat each of them as if they were in a segment of one. These organizations are important to the supplier, who will therefore take time to ensure that they understand the customer's business, collect infor-mation on product portfolio, applications, technology, production processes, purchasing policies and decision-making processes, and cultivate good relation-ships. Suppliers of specialist market research information or scientific and technical information may have this type of relationship with their customers. Other organizations, such as the large online search services, have a large customer profile that embraces both organizations and individuals. They may find it helpful to segment their markets on the basis of criteria such as size, location, usage rate, and product and service orientation.

## TARGETING

Once an organization has identified appropriate market segments, it needs to select those for which it will seek to provide a product or service. This process is known as **targeting**. An organization may adopt a single-segment strategy or a multi-segment strategy. The former allows specialization and is a good way of entering the market. This is an approach adopted, for instance, by various business information providers or CD-ROM publishers that specialize in children's games. A multi-segment strategy involves two or more segments, for which the organization develops differing marketing mixes. Most library and information services need to accommodate a number of the different market segments, and offer specialist services for groups such as children and the housebound. In other areas, there is perhaps scope for developing a more elaborate segmentation of customers, attaching priorities to these different groups. For example, academic libraries might reflect on whether all part-time students can be regarded as one segment, or whether this segment needs to be subdivided, and if so, how and for what purposes? Figure 3.2 lists some of the characteristics that might be used for segmenting academic library users. An academic library needs to decide which of these characteristics to use in order to ensure that services and marketing communication are appropriately targeted, while creating segments that are sufficiently large to be viable. Consideration of the list in Figure 3.2 demonstrates that the profile of the individual user will affect:

- the type of information sources they use;
- the purpose of using a library or a range of information sources;
- the support offered by academic tutors and the degree of independence in information use that can be anticipated;
- the type of support that they will accept, ranging from training sessions, answers to inquiries, or detailed one-to-one problem-solving sessions.

All these factors influence the services that should be available, but they also affect:

- marketing objectives, including the type of relationship that the organization seeks to build with its customers, the role of the library or information provider in the learning process, the frequency of use of library service, and the market penetration of the service;
- communication channels available for communication with users, including personalized channels such as face-to-face, telephone, and e-mail, as well as public channels such as noticeboards, leaflets, electronic newsletters and learning materials;
- messages to be conveyed to users, including messages with an emphasis on

| Segmentation characteristic | Examples of values |
|---|---|
| Mode of study | Part-time, full-time, distance learning |
| Subject of study | Science, social sciences, business, health studies, humanities |
| Age | Under 25, over 25 |
| Place of residence | Halls on campus, other student accommodation, own home |
| Year of study | 1, 2, 3, 4, sandwich year, completed students (alumni) |
| Level of study | Undergraduate, postgraduate, research |
| Disabled students | Nature of disability |

**Figure 3.2**  Some characteristics for segmenting students in an academic library

support, availability of computer facilities and study space, 24-hour access, and special services such as short-loan service.

Commercially, multi-segment targeting strategies offer potential for increasing aggregate sales or, in a public service context, increasing the range of services offered to the public, but it is particularly important to recognize that they pose more complex management challenges. At the very least, multi-segment targeting requires an understanding of the distinct benefits sought by several different segments, and the development of strategies for delivering those benefits in product packages.

Since in most information environments it is impossible to respond to the individual needs of each customer, segmentation and targeting can be important elements in understanding customer groups and building relationships with them. However, notwithstanding the value of segmentation, remember that customers are individuals too. Whilst segmentation is a useful device for categorizing users and their information needs, and associated planning and allocation of resources, it is no substitute for attention to individuals' needs and appropriate customer care. Individuals approach information products and services with a problem, to which the information can contribute a solution. Information providers need to understand the customer's problem, and in individual interactions with the customer to make judgements as to when to personalize the service. They should try to stand aside from the service delivery perspective and adopt the customer viewpoint. Customers will have a variety of problems to solve at different times and in their different roles. They will, accordingly, be members of various segments, and may use a range of information providers. They must decide which of these information providers or products is the most effective in delivering the package of benefits that they seek at a given time. They also benefit from building a relationship or gaining familiarity with a limited range of favourite information providers or sources, since this reduces the learning associated with locating and using information in different contexts.

Some practical tips on segmentation and targeting are listed in Figure 3.3.

## CONSUMER BEHAVIOUR AND DECISION-MAKING

This section focuses on the decision-making process associated with consumer buying and take-up of services and the factors that influence that process. Not all information providers are concerned whether consumers make a purchase in the conventional sense of buying. However, all information services exist for their users, and their continued existence depends on users continuing to engage

1. Identify a range of characteristics which affect the use of services or the purchase of products.
2. Consider on which of these characteristics it might be possible to collect information.
3. Consider the market research activities or the analysis required of the data in marketing information systems needed to create customer profiles.
4. Choose some segmentation variables.
5. If possible, create a customer database which records the segmentation variables for at least a significant sample of customers.
6. Using this database, or otherwise, create a profile of the segments, and an estimate of the size of each. This profile must include benefits sought and products likely to be of interest to members of the segment.
7. Choose segments for targeting.
8. Design or review key elements of the marketing mix, such as marketing objectives, product and price.
9. Design and review key elements of the promotional mix, including promotional objectives, marketing messages and communication channels.
10. Implement the marketing strategy.
11. Review the success of the segmentation approach.

**Figure 3.3**  Practical tips on segmentation and targeting

in a series of individual transactions with the service. Such transactions might mean browsing a current-awareness service, the use of a subject gateway, a visit to the coffee bar or the use of a self-service terminal. Each of these transactions can be loosely regarded as a buying episode. The steps in the consumer decision-making process outlined below are useful in emphasizing that users go through a decision-making process when they seek information or an information product. The process will be more prolonged and conscious in some types of decision-making or buying situations than in others. The cumulation of these transactions will form the basis of a relationship between the customer and the organization, as discussed in the next chapter.

Figure 3.4 shows a commonly used model of the consumer decision-making process. It involves the following stages:

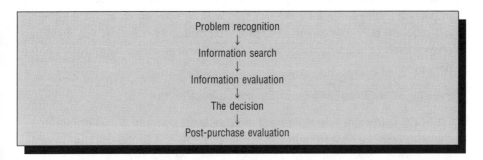

Problem recognition
↓
Information search
↓
Information evaluation
↓
The decision
↓
Post-purchase evaluation

**Figure 3.4**  The consumer decision-making process

43

- **Problem recognition**, or the identification of need. The important feature of this stage is that the process is initiated when the consumer identifies a need or a problem.
- **Information search**. At this stage the consumer searches for a solution to the need. This search typically includes an internal search covering the consumer's own previous experience, and an external search involving information-gathering from friends, colleagues and other public sources, such as consumer groups.
- **Information evaluation**, or the evaluation of alternative solutions, against selection criteria, taking into account the levels of importance of the various criteria. If one product is clearly better than all others, a decision can be made at this point.
- **The decision** is made on the basis of the criteria, but is also influenced by other random factors, as discussed below. The seller (retailer, intermediary) from whom the purchase will be made may not be selected until this stage. Here the consumer must finalize the deal. With complex purchases such as a car, final details of the contract may be agreed at this stage, or, if the purchasing or acquisition process is inconvenient, raises barriers or is delayed, the purchaser has the opportunity to reconsider their decision. Lack of appropriate assistance or other problems with the service transaction at this stage may lead the customer to refrain from making a purchase, or may affect their attitude towards making subsequent purchases or acquisitions.
- **Post-purchase evaluation**, including whether the customer is satisfied with their purchase. During this phase, cognitive dissonance, or the feeling that the purchaser has not made the correct or best decision, may arise. These doubts may be aggravated by positive marketing messages about alternative products, but may be allayed by any messages or experiences that support the purchaser's decision. Thus marketing messages, after-sales support and other interactions with the supplier are important in helping the purchaser to feel comfortable with the purchase. A positive post-purchase evaluation is important in the continuing relationship with the customer, and will influence subsequent purchase decisions. More significantly, dissatisfied customers share their dissatisfaction, and will influence other actual or potential customers.

These stages are expanded on in the example in Figure 3.5.

*REFLECT: Identify three different circumstances in which customers are likely to acquire information products. Explore the problems that might arise during the 'Purchase decision' stage of the purchase decision-making process.*

- **Problem recognition** – child with frequent homework which requires the use of basic reference sources. Insufficient time or notice to visit public library.
- **Information search** – collect information on the different types of electronic encyclopedia available on the marketplace by looking in magazines, browsing in bookshops and computer stores, scanning the Web, and talking to friends.
- **Information evaluation** – collate information about encyclopedia and learn about typical features, such as price, multimedia components, indexing, presentation and design, style of entries, extent of detail offered, availability of an atlas. Informally formulate criteria relating to acceptable price range, importance of multimedia, extended authoritative text-based entries, preference for UK publication.
- **The decision** – choose a specific title which best matches the criteria formulated in the previous stage.
- **Post-purchase evaluation** – use the encyclopedia and discover its strengths and weaknesses. Note that coverage of recent history and events is rather limited, but there are interesting botanical entries. Explore the limitations of the index, and discover that more hyperlinks between entries would be helpful.

**Figure 3.5** Example: purchase decisions for an electronic encyclopedia

This model of the decision-making process points to some important messages:

- The purchase process begins several stages before the actual purchase.
- Not all identified needs lead to a purchase, and the consumer may choose to end the process at any stage.
- Buyers may revisit certain stages and, in other circumstances, omit some stages.
- The length of the decision process may vary significantly, from minutes to years, depending on the nature of the purchase decision.

All organizations need to recognize that consumers use the decision-making process in Figure 3.4 in different ways at different times. Some of this variation is due to the differing types of purchases. Figure 3.6, for example, presents a well-

| | High-involvement purchase decision | Low-involvement purchase decision |
|---|---|---|
| Decision-making (information search, consideration of brand alternatives) | Complex decision-making | Limited decision-making |
| Habit (little or no information search, consideration of only one brand) | Brand loyalty | Inertia |

**Figure 3.6** Typology of consumer decision-making

45

established typology of consumer decision-making based on two dimensions: the extent of decision-making and the degree of involvement in the purchase.

The consumer typically performs limited decision-making in relation to products such as adult cereals and snack food, and exhibits inertia in relation to baked beans, toilet tissue and electricity. It is simply not worth spending time and effort in complex decision-making in relation to some of these products. This perspective on the varying nature of consumer behaviour leads to the development of slightly modified models of the decision-making process for different types of buying decisions:

- **Routine response behaviour** occurs with low-cost purchases, which involve little cost and decision effort. Items that are purchased frequently, such as baked beans or toothpaste, fall into this category. Regular access to databases or use of the loans service in a library might fall into this category. The marketer's role is to reinforce habits, build brand loyalty, and capture new customers by special offers and other measures that encourage impulse buying. The problem for competitors is to encourage consumers to engage in a decision-making process, rather than abide by their habitual responses.

- **Limited decision-making** occurs when a product is bought occasionally, and the purchaser finds it necessary to collect information about an unfamiliar brand or product. The purchase is important to the individual consumer, and it may relate to an item that they have not purchased in the last few years, such as a washing machine or a hairdryer. They will collect information from retailers, friends and consumer sources to inform their decision, and could be disappointed, but not devastated, if their decision is unsatisfactory in some way. With new electronic information products, such as access to CD-ROM databases or the purchase of a publication on CD-ROM, marketing messages are often necessary to move potential consumers into limited decision-making mode, so that they start to consider a new product and how it might meet their needs.

- **Extensive decision-making** occurs when purchases that are unfamiliar, expensive or infrequent are under consideration. Typically, the consumer feels exposed to a much higher risk. These purchases often involve some kind of long-term commitment. Examples are the decision-making processes associated with purchasing a car, a house or insurance products. The purchaser is motivated to collect as much information as possible, and to think carefully about decision-making criteria.

- **Impulse buying** is unplanned. Environments which encourage browsing, such as libraries and bookshops, are designed to encourage this kind of 'buying'. Impulse buying or acquisition of information products is more common where the need arises in a leisure context. Here the need or problem is often not well defined and might, for example, be expressed as: 'I need something to read while I'm on the plane'. Other contexts in which impulse 'buying' may take place are those in which the user does not know exactly what they want, or even know that they have a need, before they receive some marketing messages that suggest some new need.

All these approaches may be applied in respect of any specific service or product, since different customers may use a different approach to the same service. Thus for some, a visit to a library involves routine response behaviour, as they are regular visitors. For others, such a visit may be tantamount to impulse buying, when they find themselves in a town centre with time to kill.

Extending the typology of consumer decision-making situations in Figure 3.6, it is possible to develop a model which considers information use behaviour, as shown in Figure 3.7. Here, the concern is to specify the issues of the information seeker's inclination and motivation in relation to information-seeking. For example, a student search for information for an essay could fit into any of the categories identified in Figure 3.7, although it might be argued that the best approach would always be complex searching. The grid could also be used to categorize types of search tasks, in the sense that different information behaviour may be more appropriate for some search tasks than others in being most likely to produce optimal results (from the user's perspective). Complex searching is not required if one source, such as a public access terminal or a reference book, gives the answer. More extensive searching across several sources might verify the information or produce a more critical perspective on the original infor-

|  | High-involvement search task | Low-involvement search task |
|---|---|---|
| **Decision-making (choice of source and strategy)** | Complex searching (uses range of sources and search strategies), e.g. bibliographic search, when a comprehensive collection of literature and information is required, as over the Web, bibliographic databases, etc. | Limited searching (explores some alternatives), e.g. keeping up to date, as in scanning electronic and print sources for new developments at work, or new products for leisure purposes |
| **Habit (uses source of habit or easiest convenience)** | Quality searching (identifies one tried and tested source – searcher must be convinced that this is right), e.g. Search for facts, addresses etc. (as in a quick reference source, or a database of artefacts in a museum) | Lazy searching (takes what they find first – no evaluation), e.g. browsing, talking to friends, using an available and simple public access terminal |

**Figure 3.7** Typology of information use behaviour

47

mation, but often the user does not deem this to be necessary (even if the information professional might disagree!). The literature on consumer behaviour explores these different approaches in terms of financial, social and psychological risks. Rowley (1999) develops further the parallels between information use behaviour and the concepts associated with consumer behaviour.

## THE BUYING PROCESS IN ORGANIZATIONAL MARKETS

As stated earlier, a significant number of purchase transactions, as distinct from use interactions, in the information industry involve organizational buying. Whilst there are a number of models of the organizational buying process, there is widespread agreement that this process is more complex than its equivalent in consumer markets. Buying processes are part of the business processes in the organization, and each organization controls and expedites its purchasing activities differently. In addition, different products and services demand different approaches. Organizations have products that they buy on a routine basis (re-buy) after limited decision-making (modified re-buy) and after extensive decision-making (new task buying). Figure 3.8 shows one example of an organizational buying process which differs from the consumer buying process in two key respects:

1. **Specification** – the organization must generate a specification of the product that it requires. Components in a manufacturing process must perform the function for which they are acquired, they must meet technical and quality specifications, and they must be compatible with other components. Similar

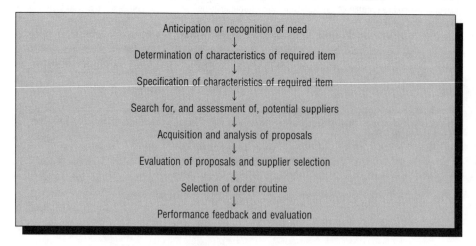

Anticipation or recognition of need
↓
Determination of characteristics of required item
↓
Specification of characteristics of required item
↓
Search for, and assessment of, potential suppliers
↓
Acquisition and analysis of proposals
↓
Evaluation of proposals and supplier selection
↓
Selection of order routine
↓
Performance feedback and evaluation

**Figure 3.8**  Model of the stages in the organizational buying process

criteria apply if a business is specifying a brief for an information or marketing research agency. Such specifications are common in the design of a library management system or other significant systems acquisition. Contracts between some organizations are now in terms of bundles of benefits, rather than specific products. Thus a rail operator may design a specification which asks for the capacity to move a certain amount of coal from A to B over the next ten years, rather than specifying the quality and quantity of the rolling stock.

2. **Supplier selection and relationships** – organizations often seek out suppliers with whom they can establish a long-term relationship. Existing suppliers may be preferred because the relationship already exists and they are a known quantity. The continuation of relationships will depend upon the supplier's ability to deliver on their promise. Some buyers adopt formal appraisal procedures for their suppliers, covering key aspects of performance such as delivery and quality.

Another aspect of the organizational buying process that makes for greater complexity is the different roles of the actors involved:

- **users** of the product or service;
- **influencers**, particularly those with previous experience of the service or some other relevant and recognized expertise, whose opinion might be sought;
- **decision makers**, who have the authority to make the use/purchase decision; they may be informed by influencers and users;
- **buyers**, who have the formal authority to buy and act as gatekeepers for purchasing within the organization. They handle the interface with suppliers.

Further complexity can be added to this model when there are collaborative arrangements which affect purchasing decisions. So, for example, if a library acquires access to online databases through its membership of a consortium, the purchasing process for those databases does not rest entirely within the library, but may be controlled by decision processes within the consortium.

## FACTORS AFFECTING CONSUMER BEHAVIOUR

Key influences on buyer behaviour derive from the product offering: the product and its benefits; the brand and packaging; the place of availability and the channels through which the product is distributed; marketing communications; reputation; and price. These factors are largely within the control of the marketer. However, a range of other personal, psychological and social factors also intervene in the consumer decision-making process. Figure 3.9 offers a list of these

**Personal**

1. Demographics, e.g. sex, age, race, ethnic origin, income, occupation, life cycle stages, e.g.
   - bachelor stage
   - newly married couples
   - full nest I – youngest child under 6
   - full nest II – youngest child 6 or over
   - full nest III – older couples with dependent children
   - empty nest I – older married couples, no children
   - empty nest II – older married couples, retired, no children
   - solitary survivor I – in labour force
   - solitary survivor II – retired

2. Situational – external circumstances at the time of the purchase decision, e.g.
   - unemployment
   - immobility due to small children
   - shortages, such as petrol or food products
   - amount of time available for decision

3. Level of involvement, e.g.
   - level of interest
   - emotional commitment and time spent searching for a product in a particular situation.

**Psychological**

1. Perception – the process of selecting, organizing and interpreting information inputs to produce meaning and how this is achieved.
2. Motives and motivation
   - Motives are the internal energy that directs a person's activities towards satisfying a need or achieving a goal.
   - Motivation is the set of mechanisms controlling movement towards goals.

3. Ability and knowledge
   - Ability in relation to information processing relating to a specific product
   - Knowledge encompasses familiarity with product and expertise

4. Attitude
   - Attitude constitutes the knowledge and positive or negative feelings about an object or activity.
   - Attitudes are learnt through experience and interaction with other people.
   - Negative attitudes, which may need special management.
   - Marketers need to measure attitudes to price, packaging, brand and location.

**Social**

1. Roles and family
Role refers to a set of actions and activities that a person in a particular position is supposed to perform, based on expectations of individuals and surrounding persons, e.g. women may adopt one or more of the roles of wife, grandmother, part-time university student. Many of the roles that an individual is called upon to adopt are related to the family.

2. Reference groups
   - A reference group is one that an individual identifies with to the extent that they adopt many of the values, attitudes and behaviours of group members. It acts as a source of information and a point of comparison.
   - Most people have several reference groups, e.g. families, friends, religious, civic and professional organizations.
   - The most influential reference group is the family.

3. Social classes
   - A social class is an open group of individuals who have similar social rank; people move in and out.
   - The criteria for grouping vary between countries, e.g. occupation, education, income, wealth, race and ethnic group, possessions.
   - It is assumed that those in the same class have common patterns of behaviour, e.g. attitudes, values, possessions, likelihood of having children.

4. Culture
   - Culture is evident in everything in our surroundings that is made by human beings, e.g. food, furniture, buildings, clothing, tools and concepts such as education, legal system, healthcare and religion.
   - Culture determines what people wear and eat, where they live and travel, and other features of their lifestyle.

**Figure 3.9** Factors influencing the consumer buying process

factors. Personal factors are those associated with the individual, such as demographic factors, lifestage, and the specific purchase decision, for example situation and level of involvement in the decision. Psychological factors are concerned with cognitive processing, based on knowledge and information processing, but influenced by attitudes and perception. Individuals do not operate alone in the decision-making process. Social factors that influence purchasing include their roles, reference groups, social class and general cultural factors. For example, purchasing is often a family process, in which it is possible to identify the different roles of initiator, influencer, decision-maker, purchaser and user. Decision-making is not divorced from the context. Further, many of these factors are outside the control of the marketer, but must nevertheless be taken into account when designing products and promotional strategies.

*REFLECT: Who are the initiators, influencers, decision-makers, purchasers and users in the following acquisition and consumption situations?*

- *A student identifying some journal articles to read to inform the development of a dissertation.*
- *A mother purchasing a children's book for her nephew.*
- *A person acquiring an article from a document delivery service over*

*the Web to provide information about the latest medical advances on diabetes, a complaint from which they suffer.*

Purchasing will also be influenced by attitudes to risk and innovation. A simple model of the diffusion of innovation is shown in Figure 3.10. This divides customers into five categories. **Innovators** will seek out new products or ideas and enjoy trying them; they want to be trendsetters. They have an important role in encouraging others to 'come on board', and are excited by the opportunity to be at the leading edge. Take-up next widens to **early adopters**, and then to the **early majority**. The remaining half of the potential customer population will respond more slowly, with **laggards** often only catching up once innovators have moved on to the next new trend. This model is a reminder that diffusion can be slow, and that there are different stages in the diffusion process. Members of a customer group will gradually transfer to new information services or, if such services replace other services and they have no option but to transfer, satisfaction with the service will only emerge gradually. Overnight successes and wholesale praise are rare events!

| | |
|---|---|
| Innovators | 2.5% |
| Early adopters | 13.5% |
| Early majority | 34% |
| Later majority | 34% |
| Laggards | 16% |

**Figure 3.10** Diffusion of innovation

*REFLECT: Choose a specific information product or service with which you have been involved. What effect might social factors have on the usage or purchase level of that product?*

Usage and loyalty are also important factors. Customers may be categorized by their usage status, for example, non-users, ex-users, potential users, first-time users and regular users. Usage rate may be heavy, medium or light. Clearly usage levels reflect previous experience with a service and, therefore, the type of decision-making and the level of information at which a decision is made. For services, a higher usage level provides an opportuntity for building a relationship with the customer. A mature relationship will include positive episodes, less satisfactory episodes, recovery, and continuing commitment and communication.

*REFLECT: What impact does previous frequency of visit or usage have in the following contexts?*

1. *Children using a children's department in a public library to select books for a project for school.*
2. *An engineer accessing an engineering-based subject gateway with a view to locating background information for a new research project.*
3. *A consumer seeking information on the Web to inform the purchase of a musical instrument.*

## CONCLUSIONS

This chapter has reviewed a range of concepts associated with the customer and consumer decision-making behaviour. An understanding of the customer and the benefits that they seek from an organization is central to the marketing concept and a marketing orientation. An analysis of customers in terms of benefits can inform effective segmentation, which in turn can act as a basis for more efficient targeting of resources. However, customer benefits are only part of the picture. The consumer decision-making process is important in determining consumer behaviour; therefore some models of the process and an analysis of the factors that determine consumer behaviour were introduced. These factors include usage levels and loyalty, concepts that are useful in seeking to critically analyse the relationship between information providers and their users and customers.

## REFERENCES AND FURTHER READING

Adcock, D., Bradfield, R., Halborg, A. and Ross, C. (1998), *Marketing Principles and Practice*. 3rd edition. London: Pitman Publishing.

Arnold, S.E. (1990), 'Marketing electronic information: theory, practice and challenges, 1980–1990', in *Annual Review of Information Science and Technology*, 25, ed. M.E. Williams. Amsterdam and Oxford: Elsenerfar, pp. 87–144.

Assael, H. (1995), *Consumer Behaviour and Marketing Action*. 5th edition. Cincinnati, OH: South Western College Publishing.

Bates, M.E. (1996), 'What's behind the pretty face?', *New User Interfaces*, **19** (4), 24–32.

Bernard, K. (1995), 'Business to business marketing', in *Marketing Theory and Practice*, 3rd edition, ed. M.J. Maker. Basingstoke: Macmillan Press, pp. 292–319.

Dibb S., Simkin, L., Pride, W.M. and Ferrell, O.C. (1994), *Marketing Concepts and Strategies*. 2nd European edition. Boston and London: Houghton Mifflin.

East, R. (1996), *Consumer Behaviour: Advances and Applications in Marketing.* Hemel Hempstead: Prentice Hall.

Engel, J.E., Blackwell, R.D. and Miniard, P.W. (1990), *Consumer Behaviour.* London: Dryden Press.

Gabbott, M. and Hogg, G. (1994), 'Consumer behaviour and services: a review', *Journal of Marketing Management,* **10** (4), 311–24.

Gabbott, M. and Hogg, G. (1998), *Consumers and Services.* Chichester: Wiley.

Mercer, D. (1996). *Marketing.* 2nd edition. Cambridge, MA: Blackwell.

Howard, J.A. and Sheth, J.N. (1969), *The Theory of Buyer Behaviour.* New York and Chichester: Wiley.

Kotler, P. (1994), *Marketing Management: Analysis, Planning, Implementation and Control.* 8th edition. Englewood Cliffs, NJ: Prentice Hall.

Rowley, J.E. (1998), 'Retailing information: the case of the online search services', *Online & CD-ROM Review,* **22** (5), 317–22.

Rowley, J. (1999), 'Towards a consumer perspective on information behaviour research', *Information Services and Use,* **19**, 289–98.

Webster, F.E. and Wind, Y. (1972), *Organizational Buying Behavior.* Englewood Cliffs, NJ: Prentice Hall.

# 4 Building customer relationships

## AIMS

This chapter is concerned with building relationships with customers. In a sense all elements of the marketing mix are concerned with relationship-building, but the focus in this chapter is on the recognition and management of two-way marketing relationships. Accordingly this chapter explores:

- the underlying concept of relationship marketing;
- some dimensions of the concept of customer loyalty; and
- the role of the service experience in building relationships.

## INTRODUCTION

> Marketing is no longer simply about developing, selling and delivering products. It is progressively more concerned with the development and maintenance of mutually satisfying long term relationships with customers. (Buttle, 1996b, p. 1)

**Relationship marketing** differs from transaction marketing (see the definitions offered in Chapter 1) in that the focus is on relationships rather than individual transactions. Gronroos (1994, p. 355) offers a general-purpose definition:

> Marketing is to establish, maintain, and enhance relationships with customers, and other partners, at a profit, so that the objectives of the parties involved are met. This is achieved by a mutual exchange and fulfilment of promises.

Perhaps one way to encapsulate the difference in emphasis between transactional and relationship marketing is in terms of the measures of success that are applied in the two approaches. In traditional marketing, market share is used to assess marketing success, whereas relationship marketing measures customer retention. Gronroos (1991) suggests that all marketing strategies lie somewhere on a spectrum from the transactional to the relational. A further difference between traditional marketing and relational marketing is that the earlier role of marketing was to create customers, whereas in relationship marketing the emphasis is on customer retention.

Relationship marketing encourages organizations to take a longer-term perspective. Investment in customer relationships creates a community for and with whom the organization can develop its products and marketing communication strategies. Enduring relationships with customers cannot be duplicated by competitors, and therefore provide a unique and sustainable competitive advantage.

Loyalty is seen as a key characteristic of relationships with customers. It can be regarded as a measure of whether the customer behaves and has attitudes that suggest a relationship with an organization. Organizations are concerned to secure as significant a loyal customer base as possible, because of the perceived link between loyalty and business performance. Loyal customers form a stable target market, and do not require the same level of marketing attention as customers who need to be wooed.

The service experience can play a significant role in shaping relationships, as it is the interaction between the customer and the supplying organization. An understanding of the service experience offers an additional insight into one important arena in which customer relationships are honed. The literature on the service experience tends to focus on episodes (although there is reference to a more longitudinal perspective in the literature on quality), whereas the literature on loyalty is concerned with the longer-term relationship between the customer and the organization.

## RELATIONSHIPS

Library and information services recognize the importance of establishing an appropriate relationship with the customer, as is evidenced, for example, in public libraries through an emphasis on customer care, and in academic libraries through the appointment of subject specialists. This commitment to customer service is well established. Nevertheless, some of the ideas from relationship marketing offer new perspectives.

Piercy (1999) encourages marketers to remember that not all customers want a relationship with their suppliers. He proposes four different categories of customers, based on the relationships that they wish to form with the supplier:

- Relationship seekers – customers who want a close and long-term relationship with suppliers

- Relationship exploiters – customers who will take every free service on offer but will still move their business when they feel like it
- Loyal buyers – customers who will give long-term loyalty, but do not want a close relationship
- Arm's-length, transaction buyers – customers who avoid close relationships and move business based on price, technical specification or innovation.

In other words, blind dedication to relationship marketing is no panacea. Marketers and managers still need to segment their markets and understand the needs of these different segments, as discussed in Chapter 3. The type of relationship that customers want is a further basis for segmentation. Organizations also segment their markets on the basis of the profitability of different customer groups, and define those segments they wish to court.

*REFLECT: Use the above categories to characterize the relationship that you as a consumer want to develop with different brands, service outlets or products.*

A number of metaphors and models have been used to explore the nature and the stages of relationships. Dwyer, Schurr and Oh (1987) suggest that supplier–customer relationships are marked by five stages: awareness, exploration, expansion, commitment and dissolution, and Christopher, Payne and Ballantyne (1991) developed the idea that there is a relationship 'ladder of customer loyalty'. The relationship progresses through the stages of: prospect, customer, client, supporter and, finally, advocate. Advocates are so deeply committed to the organization that they are not only very loyal long-term purchasers, but they also influence others through positive word of mouth.

Adcock et al. (1998) suggest the following stages in relationships: meeting, friendship, courtship and marriage, and map these stages against the customer pyramid as follows:

1. Meeting: new business prospects, previous enquiries, former customers
2. Friendship: new sales
3. Repeat customers: courtship
4. Advocate: marriage.

Czepiel (1990) explores the link between relationship-building and service encounters. He argues that relationships are developed in a number of stages:

- Accumulation of satisfactory encounters
- Active participation based on mutual disclosure and trust
- Creation of a double bond (personal and economic), and
- Psychological loyalty to the partner.

These stages include other factors that are characteristic of healthy relationships: concern (for the welfare of customers); trust (confidence that one partner has in the other's reliability and integrity); commitment (an enduring desire to maintain a relationship); and service (or the desire to provide excellent service) (Buttle, 1996b).

*REFLECT: Which of the above models of stages and types of relationship would assist in thinking about the benefits sought by your customers?*

## LOYALTY

What is loyalty? The theoretical literature on customer loyalty conceptualizes loyalty as an interaction of attitude and behaviour. In other words, loyalty (or the absence of it) is exhibited through both customer behaviour and attitude. For example, in the context of a library, loyal behaviour might be repeat and relatively frequent patronage. Such behaviour may or may not be associated with a loyal attitude, which reflects the value that a customer attaches to a library. Such attitudes may, in the case of public libraries, for instance, not necessarily lead to repeat patronage, but might provoke loyalty behaviours such as participation in a petition to resist closure of a public library service point. Dick and Basu (1994) argue that loyalty is determined by the strength of the relationship between relative attitude and repeat patronage, and that it has both attitudinal and behavioural elements. On the basis of the attitude–behaviour relationship they propose four conditions related to loyalty: loyalty; latent loyalty; spurious loyalty; and no loyalty (see Figure 4.1):

- **Loyalty** signifies a favourable correspondence between relative attitude and repeat patronage

|  |  | Repeat patronage | |
|---|---|---|---|
|  |  | High | Low |
| Relative attitude | High | Loyalty | Latent loyalty |
|  | Low | Spurious loyalty | No loyalty |

*Source:* Dick and Basu (1994).

**Figure 4.1**  Definition of categories of loyalty

- **Latent loyalty** is associated with high relative attitude, but low repeat patronage
- **Spurious loyalty** represents a low relative attitude, with high repeat patronage
- **No loyalty** is associated with a low relative attitude, combined with low repeat patronage.

There is a debate about the relationship between attitude and behaviour, and there is some support for the belief that attitude causes behaviour. On the other hand, East (1997) comments that attempts at establishing causal primacy may be unrealistic. He states that thoughts and feelings are interwoven and that changes in one component may affect others in the system.

Much of the literature on customer loyalty has looked at brand loyalty. There is a consensus (for example Zeithaml, 1981) that loyalty to service companies is likely to be easier to maintain than that to goods companies, as consumers perceive the costs of switching services to be higher. These higher costs may be associated with the acculturation or learning that is embedded in the use of services. Clearly the use of library resources involves learning about IT-based services, location of stock, and loans and reservations services. In addition, services that a customer has used regularly, such as a bank, or a library, may have generated interpersonal relationships with service agents that are an integral part of the customer's life, as discussed below. Also, switching service providers carries a risk. Due to the absence of tangibles, the risk associated with switching to a new service is perceived to be high, or, in other words, the customer cannot easily estimate the quality of the service delivery of a new service provider until they have sampled that service.

What happens in situations where customers have no choice, and are constrained to continue to use a service? Loyalty as a concept has its origins in consumer marketing, where it is assumed that customers have choice and may switch to another brand or product. What is the relevance of loyalty to marketing in other contexts, such as organizational marketing and marketing within the public sector?

Loyalty is built into supplier–customer relationships in organizational marketing. Often customers are presented with only a limited number of possible suppliers, and great inconvenience is associated with a change of supplier. On the other hand, the loss of a major business contract may spell disaster for the supplier. Relationship-building and marketing in which 'the deal' between the supplier and the purchaser is negotiated and evolves over a period time ensures loyalty; sometimes the relationship is such that the supplier actually manufactures to the purchaser's specification. Loyalty is crucial, and almost taken for granted in this context. In addition, the relationship is often more continuous and the contact more regular than in many consumer purchasing situations. Because changing the relationship between the supplier and the purchaser may have significant consequences for the continuation of business and production for both parties, loyalty is effectively embedded in their relationship.

In several other situations, particularly in the public sector, the consumer has little or no choice of provider. Here loyalty is effectively imposed, unless the customer is able to seek a substitute (for example a different leisure activity) or to turn to the private sector (for example private health care), but often the customer is at the mercy of the public service provider. Poor service might affect loyalty at the attitudinal level, but there may be no option for a change of behaviour. The customer is compelled to stay with the same supplier, and can only express discontent through being angry, uncooperative or otherwise disruptive. In these contexts, customers may respond as 'captive loyals' (Rowley, 2000). Captive customers continue to patronize a brand, service, or service outlet because they have no real choice. These customers have few opportunities for switching, or alternatively they experience what they perceive as a high switching cost (either in terms of convenience or finance). Organizations could make the mistake of viewing these customers as unlikely to switch, but captive customers can be poached by competitors with alternative offerings, or may switch when there are changes in their personal circumstances or in market structures.

## MANAGING LOYALTY

What are the factors that affect the development and maintenance of a loyal relationship? Dick and Basu (1994) propose a framework for customer loyalty that identifies the antecedents of a loyalty relationship. These antecedents can be categorized as:

- **cognitive** antecedents, which are associated with 'rational' decision-making based on informational determinants
- **affective** antecedents, associated with feelings about the product or service
- **conative** antecedents, or those associated with a behavioural disposition.

Dick and Basu (1994) argue that the management of loyalty can be viewed with reference to these factors; this would involve:

- determining the loyalty status of a target in terms of the strength of the relationship, and comparing it with competing offerings;
- identifying relevant antecedents and consequences in a given market context;
- determining the relative impact of antecedent factors and the likelihood of different consequences; and

- identifying the causal variable on which the target is underperforming compared with competitors, and from which increases in loyalty can arise.

Given these antecedents, it might be suggested that library and information services need to consider the following:

1. The **images** (brand images) **and expectations** that users hold with respect to the nature and quality of their services. This may be achieved through promotion and other communication with customers and potential customers. Customers need to be encouraged to hold strong images, value their library service, and have a clear attitude towards it.
2. The **emotions and levels of satisfaction** that are provoked by the library service. These may be enhanced through a focus on service operation efficiency (for example speed of interlibrary loans fulfilment) and customer care. Customers should enjoy and feel affection for their library.
3. The **behaviour patterns of users.** Most people are creatures of habit, and only change their behaviour or switch to another service outlet if some environmental factor provokes the change; inertia is significant. In libraries, the most important sunk cost is the learning that users need to undertake in order to be able to make effective use of the range of services offered. Such services include: the use of the photocopier; rules for borrowing and return; use of OPACs and access to the Internet through library-designed interfaces. Libraries have always suffered from low user expectations in respect of their present and future product offerings. These expectations must be raised if customers are not to be captured by attractive, competitive product offerings from new vendors entering the marketplace.

The precise agenda will be different for each information service, but managers might find the perspective offered by the loyalty literature to be a useful basis for progressing towards enhanced customer loyalty, associated positive attitudes and behaviours, and a more secure client base.

## SERVICES

Libraries, information providers, information intermediaries, online search services, database producers, software designers, interface designers and telecommunications agencies can all be regarded as providing a service. Services marketing is distinct from goods marketing due to services' unique characteristics:

1. **Intangibility** – services cannot be seen, touched, tasted, smelt or possessed. They cannot be displayed or communicated. Intangibility makes it difficult

for a customer to appreciate the service that is being offered, and to compare one service with another. On the other hand, services are rich in **experience qualities**, or those qualities that can only be assessed after purchase and consumption. They also feature **credence qualities**, qualities that cannot be assessed even after purchase and consumption.

2. **Inseparability** of production and consumption – services are normally produced at the same time as they are consumed. This consumer involvement can make it difficult to standardize and control the service.

3. **Perishability** – unused capacity in one period can rarely be stockpiled or inventoried for future periods. This also means that mass production is not an option.

4. **Heterogeneity** – people typically perform services, and do not always perform consistently. In addition, there are three parties involved in the service experience: the service agent; the customer; and other customers. Thus, again, standardization and quality are difficult to control.

These characteristics of services mean that marketing and delivery of services are interwoven and that both need special attention.

Some practical tips on marketing services are given in Figure 4.2.

## THE SERVICE EXPERIENCE

Each customer has a different experience of a library or information service. This uniqueness derives partly from the variability of service delivery, but also from the different elements in the total information service with which the customer interacts.

Often a **service experience** comprises a series of **service encounters**. In

1. Make sure that marketing occurs at all levels, from the marketing department to the point where the service is provided.
2. Allow flexibility in providing the service. When there is direct interaction with the customers, customize the service to meet their wants and needs.
3. Hire and maintain high-quality personnel and market your organization or service to them; it is often the people in a service organization who differentiate one organization from another.
4. Consider marketing to existing customers to increase their use of the service or create loyalty to the service provider.
5. Quickly resolve any problems in providing the service, to avoid damaging your organization's reputation for quality.
6. Think high-technology to provide services at lower cost. Continually evaluate how to customize the service to each customer's unique needs.
7. Brand your service to distinguish it from that of the competition.

**Figure 4.2** Practical tips on marketing services

many environments, customers can combine the service encounters into a service experience by selecting encounters and the order in which they are experienced. In a public library, for example, users can choose to use a range of information sources – the photocopier, computer-based information sources or the library staff. Each user will have a different total customer or service experience on each visit. Service providers need to be aware of these various experiences and the effect on the overall customer experience of fitting them together in different sequences. One approach to developing an understanding of the total customer experience is the use of a walk-through audit (see the practical tip, Figure 4.3).

To offer a framework for considering the extent and variety of the customer experience, three case studies are offered in the Appendix to this chapter (pp. 72–3). They are designed to demonstrate the range of customer experience within the information context. Often libraries as service outlets seek to cater for a variety of uses and users within one service. This leads to compromises that are unlikely to be tailored to the needs of the individual. The case studies also demonstrate that users do not just want information and documents from a library. They seek an experience, which may embrace leisure and recreation, culture, education, space and social interaction as well as documents and information.

Work on customer reaction to, or evaluation of, the service experience focuses on the issue of **service quality**. The construct of quality as conceptualized in the services literature and as measured by SERVQUAL (see below) centres on **perceived quality**. Perceived quality is defined as the consumer's judgement about an entity's overall excellence or superiority (Zeithaml, 1987), or a form of overall evaluation of a product. This focus on perceived quality has led to the formulation of quality that defines quality as the difference between customer expectations and customer perceptions (Parasuraman et al., 1985):

*Quality = Customer perception – Customer expectation*

A walk-through audit is one that can be conducted by managers in order to assess customer experience. Typically such audits comprise a number of questions to be answered by managers, which take the manager through the customer experience stage by stage. Questions may be asked about issues such as waiting times, ambience, quality and speed of service. The objective of such an audit is to focus on the total customer experience, rather than merely to frame a questionnaire that focuses on specific issues. The total experience, with sub-experiences in typical sequences, can be examined. Any service outlet, such as a library, would need to design a series of walk-through audit frames to reflect typical customer experiences. The exact design of these is not generally critical, provided that they reflect reasonably accurately typical customer activity and cover all the significant facilities and services offered by the library.

**Figure 4.3** Practical tips on understanding the total customer experience, with walk-through audits

In the service quality literature **expectations** are viewed as consumers' desires or wants, or what they feel a service *should* offer rather than *would* offer.

**Satisfaction**, on the other hand, is a transaction-specific measure (Oliver, 1981). The two constructs are related in that incidents of satisfaction over time lead to perceptions of good service quality.

Managing service quality is concerned with reconciling the gaps between expectations and perceptions for managers, employers and customers. The most important gap is that between customers' expectations of service and their perception of the service actually delivered, shown as Gap 5 in Figure 4.4; the work on the measurement of service quality focuses on this gap.

## SERVICE QUALITY DIMENSIONS

Service quality dimensions have evolved from work on customer reaction to the service experience and factors that influence customers' assessment of the quality of that experience. Service quality dimensions or attributes are those that contribute to consumer expectations and perceptions of service quality. Knowledge of these dimensions and, possibly, the ability to measure them, can yield insights into more effective ways of improving service quality.

Work on the service quality scale, SERVQUAL, has generated several general dimensions that apply across a number of service contexts:

1. **Tangibles** – physical facilities, equipment, appearance of personnel
2. **Reliability** – ability to perform the promised service, with dependability and accuracy
3. **Responsiveness** – willingness to help customers and to provide prompt service

| Gap 1 | The difference between what customers expect of a service and what management perceive consumers to expect |
|---|---|
| Gap 2 | The difference between what management perceives and consumers expect and the quality specification set for service delivery |
| Gap 3 | The difference between the quality specifications set for service delivery and the actual quality of that service delivery |
| Gap 4 | The difference between the actual quality of service delivery and the quality of that service delivery as described in the firm's external communications |
| Gap 5 | The difference between customers' expectations of service and the perception of service delivered |

**Figure 4.4** The service quality gaps

4. **Assurance** – knowing customers' wants, and being courteous and able to inspire confidence
5. **Empathy** – caring individual attention.

Although these dimensions have been much quoted and empirically tested, it is important to note that they provoke active debate. For example, Dotchin and Oakland (1994) observe that the range of services used by Parasuraman, Zeithaml and Berry (1985) was rather narrow. They indicate that there is little representation of types of services that provide much opportunity for consumer contact or intervention in the process. If other service categories had been included, particularly professional services, which are high in terms of opportunities for consumer intervention and adaptation, other factor groupings might have emerged associated with one or more of the incorporated dimensions: competence; credibility; security; or knowledge. Earlier work by Sasser et al. (1978) identified seven service attributes:

1. **Security**: confidence as well as physical safety
2. **Consistency**: receiving the same each time
3. **Attitude**: politeness and social manners
4. **Completeness**: availability of ancillary services
5. **Conditions**: clean and comfortable facilities
6. **Availability**: access, location, frequency
7. **Training**: propitious execution.

Such scales act as checklists for thinking about service experience and service quality, and can be useful, for example, for comparing service delivery in two different contexts, such as online and in person. They do not, however, offer much insight into customer reaction to specific elements of service delivery. For example, it was noted above that in a library and information service users normally define or personalize their own experience from a range of components on offer. Managers will often want to assess customer reaction to specific components of this customer experience, such as an enquiry service or a document delivery service. Generic scales for service quality do not operate at this level of specificity. The research and data collection approaches discussed in Chapter 9 may be employed to gather such data.

See Figure 4.5 for practical tips on managing the service experience in a library.

*REFLECT: How would you as a customer rate an information service in respect of the dimensions on one of the above scales?*

1. Train front-line staff in customer care.
2. Examine the environment, giving special attention to directional signs and the messages conveyed by the environment or any marketing communications within the library.
3. Investigate accessibility issues for any customers with disabilities and, if necessary, take expert advice.
4. Take some time to watch and gather data on how users make use of the library – are they alone or in groups? Do they browse or are they completing a specified task?
5. Specify what customers can expect in a Customer Charter or Service Level Agreement.
6. Use suggestion boxes, and consider and take action on suggestions. Inform users about how you have responded to their comments.
7. Institute a complaints procedure, and respond quickly and effectively to complaints. Service recovery is an important element in maintaining long-term relationships.
8. Smile and talk to customers – make friends!

**Figure 4.5**  Practical tips on managing the service experience in a library

## THE CUSTOMER'S ROLE IN THE SERVICE EXPERIENCE

Two alternative perspectives on the service experience, associated respectively with perceived control and scripts, may have particular applicability in interactive computer-based environments.

Psychologists have argued that in modern society, where people no longer have to concern themselves with the satisfaction of primary biological needs, the need for control over situations in which they find themselves is a major force driving human behaviour (Bateson, 1984). Perceived control can be conceptualized as a superfactor, a global index that summarizes an individual's experience with a service. The basic premise of this perspective is that during the service experience, the higher the level of control over the situation the customer feels they have, the stronger their satisfaction with the service. Similarly, it is proposed that there is a positive correlation between the service provider's experience of control and their job satisfaction. Similarly, it is important for the service firm to maintain control of the service experience, so that the economic position of the firm is not threatened. There is a three-way tension between the firm, the contract employees and the customer.

Research further shows that behavioural control or the ability to control what is actually going on is only part of the picture. Cognitive control, where consumers perceive that they are in control, is even more important. Such perceptions can be encouraged, primarily through providing appropriate information to consumers and offering them a balance between predictability and choice.

A role is defined as 'a set of behaviour patterns learned through experience and communication, to be performed by an individual in a certain social interaction in order to attain a maximum effectiveness in goal accomplishment' (Solomon et al., 1985). The central assertion is that in a service encounter customers perform roles, and their satisfaction is a function of role congruence – or whether or not the enacted behaviours by customers and staff are consistent with the expected roles. Satisfaction of both parties is likely when the customer and the service provider enact behaviours consistent with each other's role expectation. When this is not the case, both parties may be upset by the interaction. From a managerial perspective, role theory identifies two tasks:

1. to design roles for the service encounter that are acceptable and capable of fulfilling the needs of both customers and service providers; and
2. to communicate these roles to both customers and employees so that both have a realistic perception of their roles and those of their partners in the interactions.

Because role theory is not directly concerned with perceptions in the service encounter, it does not fit with concepts of service evaluation and customer satisfaction. The theory has been adapted to accommodate these issues, and developed around the idea of a script.

Script theory argues that rules, mostly determined by social and cultural values, exist to facilitate interactions in daily repetitive events, including a variety of service experiences (Smith and Houston, 1982). These rules must be acknowledged and obeyed by all participants for satisfactory outcomes. Script theory takes into account the whole service experience. Unlike roles, which are extra-individual, scripts are a function of the individual's experience and personality. Part of the job of the service provider is to uncover the script and enact it with the customer, if appropriate, or otherwise revise it in partnership with the customer.

## CUSTOMERS TOGETHER

Libraries and other information environments are often public arenas in which several customers partake of the experience in parallel. As the study of the service experience within a wide range of service environments has matured, there has been increasing recognition that customer satisfaction often depends on the customers' direct or indirect interaction as they share the service facility's physical environment (for example Bitner, 1990; Johnston, 1989). Customer-to-customer interactions can either enhance or impoverish the service experience. For example, a kind word or a pleasant smile from a fellow customer may make the service experience more enjoyable, whereas rowdy and obnoxious behaviour is likely to have the opposite effect.

Since customer-to-customer interaction may significantly affect customer satisfaction and thereby the likelihood of a return visit, it is important for service managers to be sensitive to these relationships, and the behaviours that strengthen and weaken them. More specifically, managers need to appreciate what can be done to manage or positively influence the way customers affect one another and the mechanisms by which they can support each others' experiences.

Customer-to-customer interactions may take place in a variety of contexts. Clearly, in the context of a library, the interaction may be positive either because it assists the user in the use of the information service; or the user enjoys the social exchange for its own sake. In other instances the exchange may be so negative that it overrides other elements of the experience that may be more than satisfactory. Such experiences can only be classified as potentially negative or potentially positive, since the actual nature of the experience is influenced by the perception of the customer. Note, also, that there will be occasions when some parties may perceive the interaction to be positive whilst others may perceive it to be negative. To take a simple example, as one student assists another student with change for the photocopier, these two might view the experience as supportive and positive. Others waiting in the queue for the photocopier may view the delay caused by this transaction as unwarranted, and yet other customers may find the exchange distracting.

The instinctive reaction of a service provider is to assume that customer-to-customer interactions are beyond their control. In environments such as retailing and banking, the duration of the coexistence in the shared environment may be quite short. However, in many leisure and educational environments, where the customer spends a longer period of time, typically from 30 minutes to a few hours, the significance of customer-to-customer interactions is greater and, indeed, may be more significant than customer-to-service agent interactions.

Johnston (1989) stressed the importance of the customer's role in service operations and suggested that customer management should be approached in a similar way to employee management. He identified the following customer roles:

1. Provision of explicit services in the following three forms:
   - self-services, as in supermarkets
   - services to other consumers, as in participation in a seminar or syndicate group
   - services provided for the organization, such as returning library books.
2. Creation of the environment in contexts where the atmosphere is partly due to other customers.
3. Training other customers – since customers observe each other's conduct.

4. Provision of information in specifying customer requirements and providing feedback about satisfaction.

Johnston further argued that customer management might encompass deciding upon the type of customer that is wanted and how to go about customer selection. Service organizations also need to have procedures for 'dealing with' customers who do not 'fit'.

Much of the work on customer compatibility has been conducted in physical environments. There is currently considerable interest in virtual communities and, indeed, one of the prerequisites of a portal, whether it is a commercial shopping portal or a subject gateway, is that it has a community. Commercial transactions encourage customer–supplier interaction. Communication facilities, such as e-mail, customer evaluation and messaging facilities seek to capitalize on customer-to-customer communication, but there is significant scope for development in this area before true online communities are realized in the e-marketplace.

> REFLECT: For a long time, customer compatibility in libraries was managed through the silence rule. This rule is now commonly contravened in many libraries. What other strategies for customer compatibility management can libraries employ?

## CONCLUSION

Building customer relationships develops a 'customer portfolio' alongside the organization's product portfolio, and might be viewed as the ultimate realization of marketing orientation. Organizations should consider the types of relationships that they wish to build, and the groups with whom they wish to build them. A network of relationships, including customer-to-customer relationships, contributes to the creation of a community. Organizations need marketing strategies that make this dynamic community self-perpetuating. Loyalty is an important measure of the extent and nature of relationships. The service experience offers a unique context for their development and honing. Work on service quality has offered a number of perspectives on optimum features of service environments. The future will involve tackling the issues of relationship-building, community-building and maintenance in the electronic information marketplace.

# REFERENCES

Adcock, D., Bradfield, R., Halborg, A., and Ross, C. (1998), *Marketing Principles and Practice*. 3rd edition. London: Pitman Publishing.

Bateson, J.E. (1984), 'Perceived control and the service encounter', in *The Service Encounter*, eds J.A. Czepiel, M.R. Solomon and C.F. Suprenant. Lexington, MA: Lexington Books, pp. 67–82.

Bitner, M.J. (1990), 'Evaluating service encounters: the effects of physical surrounding and employee responses', *Journal of Marketing*, **54** (2), 69–82.

Brophy, P. and Coulling, K. (1996), *Quality Management for Information and Library Managers*. Aldershot: Gower.

Buttle, F. (1996a), 'SERVQUAL: review, critique, research agenda', *European Journal of Marketing*, **30**, 8–32.

Buttle, F. (1996b), *Relationship Marketing: Theory and Practice*. London: Paul Chapman.

Christopher, M., Payne, A. and Ballantyne, D. (1991), *Relationship Marketing: Bringing Customer Service and Marketing Together*. Oxford: Butterworth-Heinemann.

Czepiel, J.A. (1990), 'Service encounters and service relationships: implications for research', *Journal of Business Research*, **20**, 13–21.

Dick, A. and Basu, K. (1994), 'Customer loyalty: toward an integrated conceptual framework', *Journal of Marketing Science*, **22** (2), 99–113.

Dotchin, J.A. and Oakland, J.S. (1994), 'Total quality management in services; part 2: service quality', *International Journal of Quality & Reliability Management*, **11** (3), 27–42.

Dwyer, F.R., Schurr, P.H. and Oh, S. (1987), 'Developing buyer–seller relationships', *Journal of Marketing*, **51**, 11–27.

East, R. (1997), *Consumer Behaviour: Advances and Applications in Marketing*. Hemel Hempstead: Prentice Hall.

Gronroos, C. (1991), 'The marketing strategy continuum: towards a marketing concept for the 1990s', *Management Decision*, **29**, 7–13.

Gronroos, C. (1994), 'Quo vadis, marketing? Towards a relationship marketing paradigm', *Journal of Marketing Management*, **10**, 347–60.

Johnston, R. (1989), 'The customer as employee', *International Journal of Production and Operations Management*, **9** (5), 15–23.

McKee, B. (1991), 'Choosing quality: a management agenda for public libraries', *Local Government Policy Making*, **18** (1), 47–52.

Oliver, R. (1981), 'Measurement and evaluation of satisfaction process in retail settings', *Journal of Retailing*, **57** (Fall) 25–48.

Parasuraman, A., Zeithaml, V. and Berry, L. (1985), 'A conceptual model of service quality and its implications for future research', *Journal of Marketing*, **49** (Fall), 41–50.

Piercy, N.F. (1999), 'Relationship marketing myopia', *Marketing Business*, October, 40–41.

Rowley, J.E. (2000), 'Understanding loyalty and loyals: the customer perspective', *Proceedings of the Academy of Marketing 2000*. University of Derby: AM.

Sasser, W.E., Olsen, R.P. and Wyckoff, D.D. (1978), *Management of Service Operations*. Boston: Allyn & Bacon.

Smith, R. and Houston, M. (1982), 'Script-based evaluations of satisfaction with services', in *Emerging Prospective in Services Marketing*, eds L. Berry, G.L. Shostack and G. Upah. Chicago: American Marketing Association, pp. 59–62.

Solomon, M.R. et al. (1985), 'A role theory perspective on dyadic interactions: the Service Encounter', *Journal of Marketing*, **49**, Winter, 99–111.

Zeithaml, V.A. (1981), 'How consumer evaluation processes differ between goods and services', *Marketing of Services*. Chicago, IL: American Marketing Association.

Zeithaml, V. (1987), *Defining and Relating Price, Perceived Quality and Perceived Value*. Request No. 87–101. Cambridge, MA: Marketing Science Institute.

# APPENDIX: SOME CUSTOMER EXPERIENCES OF LIBRARY AND INFORMATION SERVICES

## CASE STUDY 1: A PUBLIC LIBRARY USER SEEKING LEISURE READING

Mrs Brown finds a parking space close to her local branch public library, pays for the parking ticket and walks to the library. She enters the library at 10.45 on a Saturday morning, accompanied by her two school-age children. They join the queue at the counter in order to return the books they borrowed two weeks ago. They queue for three minutes and meanwhile chat to neighbours who are also in the queue. Child 1 disappears to examine the children's books, whilst Child 2 is waiting to help to place the books for discharge on the counter. When their turn arrives, the assistant points out that fines of 20p are due on the books because they are one day overdue. Mrs Brown pays the fines. She then moves on to the children's section to check that Child 1 is fruitfully engaged and not disturbing other people. Child 2 is seeking some information for homework in an encyclopedia. Mrs Brown assists with the use of the index and helps to locate the appropriate section. Together Mrs Brown and Child 2 visit the photocopier, only to discover that they do not have the correct change. A visit to the change machine rectifies the situation, and after examining the photocopier instruction they copy two pages. Meanwhile Child 1 has selected five books, but can only borrow four. Negotiations ensue to reduce the set of books to four. Child 2 goes to select their own books. Mrs Brown heads for the adult science fiction section, with Child 1 following, and asking to 'get my book stamped'. After a quick browse of the science fiction stock, Mrs Brown selects some reading for herself and her husband. She then browses through leaflets on display about local activities. They then all three queue for a short while to have their books issued and leave the library at 11.20 to return to their car.

## CASE STUDY 2: A STUDENT USER SEEKING READING FOR AN ESSAY

Mr Green enter the university library at 2.00 after a light lunch with friends in the student refectory. He consults the OPAC to check the locations and availability of items on the reading list that he has been issued in respect of an assignment which is due in three days' time. A number of the books on the reading list have already been borrowed by other more diligent students who are tackling the same assignment, so Mr Green conducts a wider subject-based search on the OPAC to identify other potentially useful books. With a list of these titles and their shelfmarks, Mr Green visits the shelves, and is successful in locating some, but not all, of the books he requires. He then visits the short-loan collection to ascertain whether the study packs that have been prepared by his lecturer are available. These are all booked, so he books one for 10.00 am the following day. He takes the books that have been located in the study area and settles down to obtain a broad grasp of the key issues of the assignment. After browsing through the books he selects three for borrowing and reads short sections in and takes notes from two other books. After an hour of study and approximately two hours in the library Mr Green decides that it is time for a coffee. Leaving his work in the library, he leaves the library and visits the nearest student coffee bar, to return approximately 20 minutes later, having also visited the toilets on his way back. He then seeks some of the periodical articles that are on his reading list. Once he finds these he decides to photocopy three of them. The photocopier is busy, and he needs to wait 15 minutes. By now it is getting towards the end of the afternoon. Mr Green returns journal volumes to the shelves, and takes the books that he intends to borrow to the issue desk, together with the notes and photocopies he has made. He now has collection of materials that he will take home and use to study further in the evening.

## CASE STUDY 3: A BUSINESS MANAGER SEEKING INFORMATION ON COMPETITORS FROM A BUSINESS LIBRARY

Mrs Black telephones the information services associated with the business library with which her organization is a registered user. She requests financial profiles for three of her organization's competitors. After a brief 'reference interview' during which the information officer seeks to clarify the question, the information officer undertakes to locate the required information and to fax details in about half an hour. Half an hour later Mrs Black receives a fax giving the summary details as requested. At the end of the month, the organization receives a monthly invoice for services used.

# 5 Information products

## AIMS

This chapter explores the nature of information products. It:

- identifies examples of information products;
- explores the definitions and applications of the concept of core, actual and augmented products;
- identifies the central role of product in defining relationships between customer and supplier;
- reviews the unique features of information as a product;
- introduces the product lifecycle; and
- explores the management of product portfolios.

## THE FIRST STEP

The product is the key component in the marketing exchange. Successful marketing rests on the ability of the product to deliver a solution to the customer's problem, or to deliver the bundle of benefits that a customer seeks (Webster, 1994). The range of products in the information marketplace is vast, and to make the picture yet more complex, there is a myriad of different relationships between these products. This section starts with simple definitions and examples, but the next two sections demonstrate that the definition of the product is not as straightforward as it might first appear. The ideas presented in these sections are designed to encourage thinking about the nature of information products, and specifically those products offered by your organization. So, what is an information product?

> An information product is any product (either good or service) whose core or primary product is information or knowledge.

75

This statement could be read as an invitation to explore the nature of information and the relationship between information and knowledge. There are multiple definitions of information which have their origins in a variety of disciplines (Rowley 1998), and whilst all information professionals should be acquainted with the multifarious nature of information and the impacts that it may have for individuals, organizations and societies, for the purposes of this book we are interested in information as it is packaged into information products.

Returning to the definition of product that was used in Chapter 2:

> A product is a physical good, service, idea, person or place that is capable of offering tangible and intangible attributes that individuals or organizations regard as so necessary, worthwhile or satisfying that they are prepared to exchange money, patronage or some other unit of value in order to acquire it.

This definition reminds us that products include ideas, goods and services. Figure 2.1 (p. 17) listed some examples of information products. Any one information provider will offer a subset of such products and services. Figure 5.1 lists the products offered by Engineering Information Inc. (Ei). These include several products which package data from a common database for specific audiences, products that are available over the Internet, and products that are available in print form or on CD-ROM. Ei products include different types of documents, such as reports, conference proceedings and standards, and have

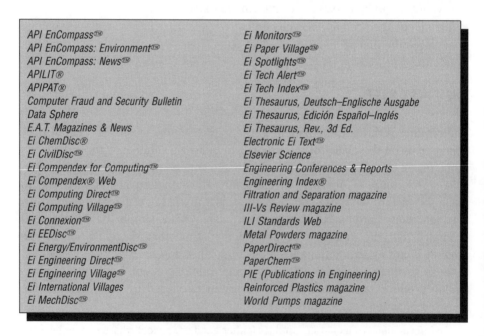

API EnCompass™
API EnCompass: Environment™
API EnCompass: News™
APILIT®
APIPAT®
Computer Fraud and Security Bulletin
Data Sphere
E.A.T. Magazines & News
Ei ChemDisc®
Ei CivilDisc™
Ei Compendex for Computing™
Ei Compendex® Web
Ei Computing Direct™
Ei Computing Village™
Ei Connexion™
Ei EEDisc™
Ei Energy/EnvironmentDisc™
Ei Engineering Direct™
Ei Engineering Village™
Ei International Villages
Ei MechDisc™

Ei Monitors™
Ei Paper Village™
Ei Spotlights™
Ei Tech Alert™
Ei Tech Index™
Ei Thesaurus, Deutsch–Englische Ausgabe
Ei Thesaurus, Edición Español–Inglés
Ei Thesaurus, Rev., 3d Ed.
Electronic Ei Text™
Elsevier Science
Engineering Conferences & Reports
Engineering Index®
Filtration and Separation magazine
III-Vs Review magazine
ILI Standards Web
Metal Powders magazine
PaperDirect™
PaperChem™
PIE (Publications in Engineering)
Reinforced Plastics magazine
World Pumps magazine

**Figure 5.1** Products available from Engineering Information Inc.

different subject scope, such as Engineering, Computing and Metal Powders. In addition, the product portfolio includes tools, such as thesauri, that support the use of the other information products available from Ei. Figure 5.2 shows the information services available from a major university library, as presented on its Web page.

In Figure 2.1 (p. 17) we listed some different kinds of services. Some exist to provide access to the goods, such as books and periodicals, whilst others act as umbrella services for a set of more 'minor' services. For example, a photocopying service is commonly offered within an academic library. Most organizations offer a collection of information services and goods. Clarity about the products that an organization offers to its customers is essential, and where, as is often the case, different packages of products are being offered to different market segments, the product offering should be designed to suit those segments. In particular, even if a given market segment is being offered a product which draws on several different departments, the consumer should not be aware of this organizational structure from the way in which they experience either marketing communications or operations

As far as customers are concerned, **products are bundles of benefits**. Figures 5.3 and 5.4 illustrate the important concept of benefits for an information product and an information service, respectively.

## CORE, ACTUAL AND AUGMENTED PRODUCTS – WHAT IS REALLY THE PRODUCT?

Figure 5.5 defines products as having three levels: core, actual and augmented. These are now defined in detail:

- The **core product** is what actually meets the consumer's needs. In this

| | |
|---|---|
| General Information | Reprographics |
| Opening hours, staff, facts and figures | Library News |
| Library Collections | SCONUL Vacation Access Scheme |
| Including the EDC, special and general collections | Infobytes |
| Issue Desk | BUCS Help Desk |
| Enquiry Services | National Cataloguing Unit for the Archives of |
| Learning Support Services | Contemporary Scientists (NCUACS) |
| Distance Learning Service | UK Office for Library and Information Networking |
| Inter-Library Loans | (UKOLN) |
| Library Article Request Service | MSc in Information and Library Management |

**Figure 5.2** Services from Bath University Library

*Literature Online* was launched in 1996 to international acclaim from scholars and librarians. It brought together Chadwyck-Healey's full-text databases in English and American literature, previously only available individually on CD-ROM, and enabled users to search them all together, giving easy access to more than 250,000 works of poetry, prose and drama. To these full-text databases it added a dictionary and a master index of Websites related to literature in English. *Literature Online* broke new ground in electronic publishing and set the standard for the delivery of scholarly materials over the Internet.

**Features**
*Literature Online* now provides:

- direct access to over 260,000 texts spanning 1,400 years
- comprehensive material for the study of almost every period and genre of English literature
- twentieth-century material by the major authors of the last 100 years
- integration of all primary and secondary sources, accessible from a single search
- comprehensive information about the top 1,000 most widely studied authors, including biographies, works by them and works about them
- powerful search and reference tools
- links to further Web resources, selected for their quality and range of useful literary materials
- quick and easy site navigation
- flexible search fields for refining your enquiries
- the complete *Annual Bibliography of English Language and Literature* from 1920 to today and the new *Literary Journals Index Full Text* covering 200 literary journals

**Benefits**
With *Literature Online* you can:

- perform searches across all genres or just those you are interested in
- search simultaneously across all primary works and secondary sources
- view the full text of any work in the database
- look up the details of an author from a collection of 1,000 biographies
- find a full list of the works of a particular author
- find a full list of works about a particular author
- discover who wrote a particular work
- find out which genres were employed by particular authors
- learn more about literary movements an author belonged to
- identify relevant periodical articles, book reviews and monographs published between 1920 and today
- read selected articles from current literary journals

**Figure 5.3** *Literature Online* – the difference between product features and benefits

context, the core product is always information. In most cases the user seeks information on a specific subject, and to fulfil a specific purpose (leisure, education, writing a report, undertaking a market research exercise). In the commercial context of a can of baked beans, the core product is the baked beans.

- The **actual product** is what is delivered to the consumer. For information

- Access (lifts, assistance)
- Reserved car parking spaces
- Toilet facilities accessible to people with mobility impairments
- Staff help with photocopying
- Book retrieval service
- Material in different formats
- Reading service
- Flexible loan periods

**Figure 5.4** 'Benefits' offered to users with disabilities in Manchester academic libraries

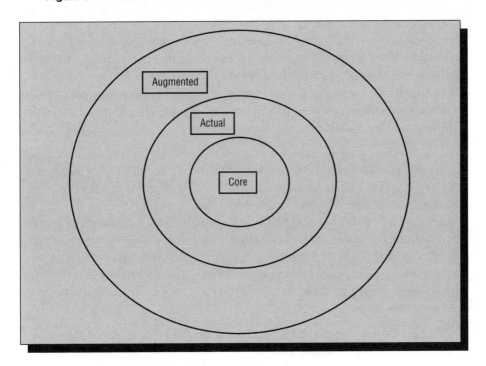

**Figure 5.5** Core, actual and augmented products

products this will be the various ways in which information can be packaged into products, such as books and journals, or into a service, such as database access. In the case of baked beans, the actual product is the can of beans (the beans of a given quality, colour and flavour and the can of a specified size, with a label, and the branding and information that is printed on the label). In other words, brand names, design and style, packaging, and characteristics such as size are typical features of the actual product. In the case of information products the actual product may have structuring, indexing, quality, presentation, design, style and physical characteristics. For example,

79

an entry in an encyclopedia in print form may contain similar information to the same entry in electronic form, but layout, presentation, and the ways in which the information can be manipulated may vary. In addition, the electronic version may have other multimedia elements, such as a video clip which allows a multidimensional expression of the information.

- The **augmented product** includes any other features that constitute part of the product and add value to the exchange. For the can of baked beans, augmentation is limited because the product is simple, but typically includes a quality guarantee. With more complex products, such as a computer, the augmented product includes a warranty, after-sales service, installation arrangements and customer help-lines. The augmentation in an information product is the added-value components. For an online search service, the actual product might be database access through a user-friendly interface. The augmented product might embrace a document ordering and delivery option, an SDI (selective dissemination of information) service and training seminars. Some elements of the augmented product may be charged for; others may be available free.

In many product categories, the boundaries between core, actual and augmented are not fixed for all time, and are, in any case, more difficult to draw for services (and probably for electronic information products) than for physical products. Organizations in the same marketplace all share the same core product. They differentiate themselves on the basis of the actual product. In the many marketplaces where the opportunity for innovation is limited (all washing machines exhibit a similar range of washing cycles), differentiation may be on the basis of the augmented product. This augmentation may be added by the producer, with a view to achieving differentiation from the products of other producers, as well as by the retailer.

*REFLECT: How might a subject gateway on the Web augment the databases to which it provides access?*

Generally, the core product will be coincident with one of the core businesses of the organization, but with the advent of e-commerce, many more organizations are redefining their role and entering the knowledge business. Thus an organization such as a supermarket, whose core service is retailing, may find that e-commerce activities allow them to generate 'rich' customer information. If they choose to market this information to other organizations, then that information becomes one of their core products.

*REFLECT: What are the core, actual and augmented products offered by an academic library when it makes a collection of electronic journals available to its users?*

Chapter 4 explored the concept of the customer experience in a public library: each user has a different experience of a library depending on which of the offered services and products they use. The consumer has scope for personalizing the service: the benefits that they derive from an information service are unique to their needs, the route that they choose to satisfy those needs, and their success in travelling that route. In marketing such an experience, a library would normally choose to market the institution and its facilities. As discussed further in Chapter 7, promotion may focus on specific products and services, or on cultivating awareness of and a positive image for the organization. Marketing messages (including negative publicity) about the organization will affect the products and services that the organization offers, and vice versa. On the other hand, whilst all customers and users want to know that the organization with which they are doing business is reputable, professional, and visible in the marketplace, their real concern is with the services and products they can obtain from the organization, and the benefits they can derive from those products.

## THE PLURI-SIGNIFIED PRODUCT

Recent thinking about the relationship marketing paradigm has caused marketers to revisit the concept of product, and to explore the true nature of the core product from a consumer perspective, rather than from the producer perspective which is dominant in the model discussed above.

The most basic level of the product is the core product, or the fundamental service or benefit that the customer is buying. For example, in the case of a hotel, the guest is actually buying rest and sleep, but this is achieved through the purchase of the actual or generic product, which may be the rental of a hotel room. Saren and Tzokas (1998) argue that core benefits cannot be predetermined by the marketer, but that core needs have been replaced by a complex constellation of 'needs activities'. So for example, hotels have evolved as conference centres, fitness and leisure centres, and locations for dining and wedding receptions. This concept of a constellation of needs activities is consistent with the proposition that consumers do not consume products for their material utilities but, instead, consume the symbolic meaning of those products (Baudrillard, 1988). This symbolic meaning of products is not fixed, but free-floating, and each individual may ascribe different and inconsistent cultural meanings to a product (Mick and Buhl). Saren and Tzokas (1998) introduce the concept of the pluri-signified product, in which 'the product is the outcome of a continuous tripartite signification process between buyers, suppliers, and the "object"'. Further, 'the relationship between the three actors (buyer–supplier–object) defines the product' (p. 451). The product itself does not exist independently of this tripartite relationship. It is created and becomes at any point in time realized, interpreted and reinterpreted by means of the continuously negotiated relationship between these three actors in what is traditionally termed the 'market exchange process'.

These concepts suggest a perpetual evolution of the concept of product, and emphasize the need to consider not only the organization's definition of the product, but also how the customer perceives, and interacts with, the organization's offering to satisfy the needs they bring to the interaction. As a key component in the interchange or relationship between customer and supplier, the product is continually subject to redefinition, in order to respond to the dynamic nature of the complex bundles of benefits that customers seek from products.

## INFORMATION AS A PRODUCT

This book focuses on the information products defined by organizations, many of which will be a combination of goods, service and information components. Freiden et al. (1998) argue that the unique nature of information as a product demands a new approach to marketing, which they describe as **information marketing**. They stress that it is important to understand the unique nature of information as a product. The characteristics of information are particularly likely to influence information products, in which the core product is information, but will also have an impact on any other products that use information as a part of their offering. One of the challenges of presenting information as a product package is to overcome these inherent characteristics. For example, although information may have no intrinsic value, customers need to be persuaded that in the contexts in which they are acquiring it, information does have value. Further, if a price for the exchange is to be agreed, the values that the supplier and customer, respectively, attach to the product must coincide.

Key to the marketing of information is the early recognition that its exchange is quite different from that of other commodities. Transmitting information involves no loss, so that the usual means of control of resources – legal protection, secrecy and monopoly – are inapplicable here. In addition, the value of information to the purchaser is not known or verifiable until it has been received, and it may be many months or years until a purchaser fully appreciates the value of the original information.

Discussion of the special nature of information products can range through some of the characteristics that are unique to information, to those that have been used to differentiate between goods and services: perishability; homogeneity; inseparability; and intangibility (based on Eaton and Bawden, 1991 and Freiden et al., 1998):

1. **Value is contextual** Information has no intrinsic value. Its value depends upon its context and its use by particular users on specific occasions, and cannot be determined in advance. It is also difficult to predict how the value will change over time. In general a distinction should be made between cost and value, but the relationship between these is ill defined.

2. **Reproducibility and multiplicability** Information is not lost when it is given to others, although its usefulness for particular purposes may be reduced. Nor does it diminish when 'consumed'; its sharing and transmission may, and indeed almost always will, cause its increase. In economic terms, then, information has a self-multiplicative quality, since its exchange does not necessarily imply redistribution, loss or consumption. This characteristic of information is supported by its reproducibility. Information may be easily copied for and by other consumers, using photocopying and electronic technologies. Further, information can be transformed from one medium into another, as when it is scanned into electronic databases, or printed out from them.

3. **Interactivity** Information is a dynamic force for change to the systems within which it operates and must be viewed within an organization as a formative, organizing entity rather than as an accumulated stockpile of facts. Information is not, then, something that an organization acquires in the way that it might acquire other products. It is often acquired so that it can be integrated with information from other sources, and either used to inform decision-making, plans and actions, or to create other information products. At an individual level, information is integral to the learning process, and its use enhances the learner's cognitive ability to absorb other information.

4. **Repackageability** Information comes in many different forms, and is expressed in many ways. For example, one unit of information, such as a reference, may be located in a range of sources, and these sources themselves may differ in nature. Several different products may be generated from one database to meet the needs of various audiences. Since new knowledge is created from existing knowledge, it can be difficult to decide when information is original or different. Differentiation may depend on the level of analysis of the information, and the purpose for which it is required.

5. **Delivery and technology** In the context of electronic information, technology constrains and facilitates the delivery of information. New telecommunications technology with greater bandwidth and storage capacities supports additional information flow, and generates greater demands for the structuring and filtering of information. Further, the user may not only pay for the information, but also for the use of the facilities, such as retrieval software, that are crucial in determining whether a user finds the appropriate information and thus in influencing customer satisfaction. The user's ability to use the tools that

provide the interface to the information determines their experience of the product.

6. **Perishability** One characteristic that distinguishes between goods and services is perishability. Goods have varying levels of perishability, but services only have value when they are produced and consumed. Information, on the other hand, is essentially non-perishable. Information does not deteriorate over time (permanence), although the medium in which it is stored may do so. On the other hand, the value of information can vary with time. Information can have multiple lifecycles, as ideas come into, move out of, and finally come back into, fashion. The uncertainty associated with how long information is of value after it has been created, distributed and even purchased provokes the collection and archiving of information. Some documents and the information that they contain may be required many years after they were first published. On the other hand, some information becomes obsolete, and different kinds of information have different lifespans (obsolescence). Information, then, has various levels of perishability, like goods, but unlike services.

7. **Homogeneity** Goods demonstrate a high level of homogeneity, but services, due to the personal elements in delivery, are much less consistent. Information products are at the extreme end of the homogeneity spectrum, since each copy is identical to each other copy, and to the original. Managers of information have the opportunity to emphasize a standardized, quality-controlled product.

8. **Inseparability** refers to the physical and institutional distance between the originator of the product and the final consumer. Goods may pass through several intermediaries between manufacture and purchase by the customer. Services, on the other hand, are inseparable because the producer and the consumer need to interact in creating, delivering and consuming the service. Information is more akin to a good than a service in that it is produced, stored, transported and can exist without being consumed. Information must be distributed, either through telecommunications networks or through bookshops, libraries and other intermediaries.

9. **Tangibility** refers to the product's physical properties and the extent to which it can be seen, felt, heard, tasted or smelt. Goods have physical attributes such as size and colour, whereas the performance of a service is largely intangible. The only tangible element of information rests with the medium through which it is conveyed. Thus information products, such as books and magazines, are tangible, although the information that they contain is not.

The discussion above relates to information itself, but also starts to touch on how information is packaged into products and services. Whilst these features are important, because information is threaded through all the products in the information industry, the nature of the product and, accordingly, marketing options depend to a significant extent upon the way in which the service, good and information components are drawn together to create the information product.

## QUALITY INFORMATION

When information is packaged into products, the quality of those products will be judged by some of the underlying characteristics of good information. The characteristics that form the basis for the quality assessment of goods and services are widely recognized. Consumers tend to judge the perceived quality of many goods by criteria such as performance, product features, conformance with specification, reliability, durability, serviceability, and fit and finish (Garvin, 1984). Similarly, the quality of services can be evaluated by the criteria of reliability, empathy, responsiveness, assurance and tangibility (Parasuraman, Zeithaml and Berry, 1985). The characteristics of good information define benefits that are often sought by those acquiring it. They include objectivity, explicitness, currency, relevance, structure and systems.

### OBJECTIVITY

The debate associated with the objectivity of information is relevant to all types of information and all disciplines. All information is a product of the societal, organizational and cultural environment in which it is created. However, the issue of objectivity has been most hotly debated in the social sciences. Social science researchers and information users are acutely aware of the difficulties associated with creating a shared reality, which could be regarded as valid and transferable objective information. Science and technology, on the other hand, often investigates problems and environments where experiments can be repeated under similar conditions to give consistent results and consensus on what can be described as objective information. Related to the issue of objectivity are those of reliability and accuracy. **Accuracy** means that information is correct. **Reliability** implies that the information is a true indicator of the variable that it is intended to measure. Users often judge reliability of information on the basis of the **reputation** of the source from which it has been drawn.

### ACCESSIBILITY AND FORM

Accessibility refers to the availability of information to potential users. The factors that contribute to accessibility may be of significance here, for example the form and style of the storage and communication media. Form refers to the mode and medium through which information is made available to users. Information may be stored and communicated via people, print or electronic media. Marketers should make information available to users in the form that they prefer; this will often lead to the replication of information in different forms. The style must be understandable by users. The user's information environment, language and user preferences all influence the success with which the message is received.

## RELEVANCE

Information available to an individual must be appropriate to the task in hand; that available to an organization must be relevant to its current direction, vision and activities. Relevance means that the information meets requirements. It can be assessed in relation to many of the other characteristics listed in this section, such as currency and accuracy, but may be judged specifically in terms of level of detail and completeness. **Completeness** is normally judged in relation to a specific task or decision; all the material information necessary to complete a specific task must be available. In addition, the **level of detail**, or **granularity**, of the information must match that required by the task and the user.

## CURRENCY

Currency and **lifespan** of information are important for two reasons: some information may supersede other information; and the most current information is required (outdated information must be discarded). Each type of information has its own lifecycle and rate of obsolescence. At one end of the time-scale there is a core of relatively stable information for each discipline, such as the way in which the heart functions, or the process for the refining of steel. Other information is outdated within hours. Examples include the weather report and international exchange rates. The challenge is to be able to recognize the positioning on a time-scale of specific information and to manage that information accordingly.

## STRUCTURE AND ORGANIZATION

All information has a structure. At the individual cognitive level, the brain holds associations between specific concepts. This cognitive structure is reflected in the way in which individuals structure information in their communications in the form of verbal utterances, text and graphical representations. Some disciplines have inherent structures: biology, for example, is organized to reflect the structure of living matter, and documents on biology can be arranged consistent with this structure. Newspapers group information into categories, such as news, politics and sport. The two important features of structure are:

- the way in which items are grouped into categories; and
- the relationships between these categories.

## THE PRODUCT LIFECYCLE

The product lifecycle (PLC) model suggests that products go through a cycle comprising four stages: introduction; growth; maturity; and decline. This lifecycle can be applied to an individual product (a specific title on CD-ROM), a brand, or a product class (CD-ROMs). Marketing actions might depend upon the stage that a product has reached in the PLC, which can therefore be a useful guide in thinking about the future for a product, and the characteristics of each stage in the PLC. Unfortunately, analysis based on the PLC is problematical, because after a short period following the introduction of a product, it is difficult to assess the stage that a product has reached. In addition, it is every business's objective to maintain a product in the growth phase of the lifecycle for as long as possible. Nevertheless the model offers some useful perspectives on the marketing strategies that are appropriate at each stage in the PLC.

### INTRODUCTION

During this phase, sales are relatively low, and profit will be low or negative, but if the product is to survive to the growth stage, this stage is likely to require a significant investment of marketing resources. The marketer's priority is to generate widespread awareness of the product among the target segment, and to stimulate trial. If the product is truly innovative, for example a technological innovation, there may be no competition, but there is the additional problem of establishing a demand for this new category of product. When a new product is an improved version of an existing one, entering an existing marketplace, success depends significantly on the USP, and the effectiveness with which this can be communicated.

### GROWTH

The growth stage should witness a significant increase in sales and profits; product awareness has improved, and, depending on the product, there may be repeat purchases. However, during this stage, competitive pressure will mount as competitors respond with their offerings. Building a loyal customer community and market share is a key issue at this stage. Towards the end of it, the organization should have collected significant information about the strengths and weaknesses of the product and customer reaction. This information can be used to inform the next phase of product innovation.

## MATURITY

The growth rate levels off, and a stable set of loyal repeat buyers should have emerged. Customers will leave this group, and others will join, but sales and profits will hold steady. There is a high degree of customer understanding of the product, and customers have decided what they like about it. Sales may decline if customers switch to alternative products. Marketing efforts should focus on retention of a loyal customer base, and increased marketing expenditure may be necessary, as all businesses seek to retain loyal customers. Eventually the stability of the mature phase will pass, and sales will go into decline. This may be provoked by a weakening competitive position or by changing customer expectations of products in the class, which signals the need for further innovation.

## DECLINE

When decline is on the horizon, the organization must decide whether to seek to rejuvenate the product, perhaps by changing the product, its image or the target market. If rejuvenation is not an option, and the decline has arisen from market conditions, the only marketing intervention available is the development of a new product.

Although the product lifecycle offers some useful ideas on marketing strategies, it has a number of limitations. The length of the product lifecycle will vary for each product, and it is very difficult to identify when a product moves from one phase to another. In addition, for different products the shape of the PLC will vary depending upon the maximum sales levels that the product achieves, and the length of each phase. For example, a product failure may never achieve growth, a fashion product may have a rapid growth and an equally rapid decline, with a virtually non-existent mature phase, but other products may linger in the mature phase for twenty or thirty years.

*REFLECT: Name some:*
- *consumer products that have been in the mature phase for several years;*
- *information products that have been in the mature phase for several years.*

## PACKAGING AND LABELLING

Packaging and labelling are part of the product that have both functional and communication purposes. Packaging has limited relevance in parts of the information industry, but book jackets and CD and video cases are important. Packaging is often the consumer's first point of contact with the product and, in the information products described previously, often plays a significant role in determining whether the customer proceeds with a purchase, or the user looks further into the contents of the document.

Packaging is any container or wrapping in which the product is offered for sale. Its functional role is to protect the product in storage, shipment and, sometimes, in use. It may have several layers, and from the consumer's perspective, it should be convenient and easy to use. Packaging also has a very important role in communicating product information (contents), communicating a brand image, attracting attention and, in general, determining whether the consumer will explore the product further. Some of these objectives may be achieved through the container that forms the packaging, whilst other information and messages may be communicated through labels. Labels often carry warnings and instructions.

## PRODUCT PORTFOLIOS

Most organizations offer a variety of products and variations of each individual product, perhaps designed to meet the needs of different product segments. Figure 5.2 (p. 77) listed the services offered by Bath University Library. The **product mix** is the sum of all the products offered by an organization. On occasions it can be useful to divide this mix into groups. For example, a **product line** is a group of products that are closely related to each other, and a **product item** is an individual product or brand, which has its own unique features and benefits. A product line normally consists of a number of product items.

In a dynamic environment, products in the product mix will be at different stages in their PLC; the product mix will not be static. The management challenge is to create a dynamic product portfolio that embraces a balanced mix of products at different stages in their lifecycle. Managing a product portfolio involves:

- maintaining and supporting established products so that they continue to perform well in the marketplace;
- modifying and adapting existing products to take advantage of technological and other marketplace developments;
- deleting old products that are in decline;

- developing and introducing new products to maintain or improve sales, and to provide a foundation for the future.

The first of these is achieved through the manipulation of various elements in the marketing mix to ensure that the product is regarded as attractive relative to its competitors in the target market. In what follows we reflect briefly on some of the other areas of product portfolio management.

## MODIFYING EXISTING PRODUCTS

Modification of existing products is often associated with repositioning or, in other words, changing the characteristics of the product that differentiate it from its competitors. Such repositioning may be triggered by changing customer needs, developing technology or new offerings from competitors. Repositioning and product modification are often focused on one or more of: quality; design (from an aesthetic perspective); and technical performance.

Another approach is not to change products, but to develop the product range, using existing products as the basis for new ones.

## DELETING PRODUCTS

Once products have reached the final stage of their lifecycle they are candidates for deletion. The decision to delete products from the range is often difficult, and there may be legitimate reasons for retaining a product even if it does not attract much customer attention. Some products and services may provide an infrastructure for the delivery of more recently introduced products, and organizations may be keen to retain a wide product range. Similarly, when production processes of products are interlinked (as with the multiple products from a database), it can be difficult to cost the production of specific products in the range and to assess whether they are making a sufficient contribution.

## DEVELOPING A NEW PRODUCT

If product modification is not sufficient, organizations may engage in the development of new products. The extent of newness can vary from a completely new technical innovation, launched as a distinct product, to a product that, whilst new to the organization, may already have an established niche in the marketplace. Products that are new to the market must win customer interest and confidence. Customers must be persuaded that they need this new product that they have done without up to now. Significant risks are associated with this level of innovation, because development and marketing costs are likely to be high, and customers need convincing. Success with significant innovations requires a large commitment to research and development, and a proactive approach to innovation. A lower-risk alternative is to develop an innovation, but using a familiar core product concept. An example might be the first mobile phone to access the Internet. Customer interest is easier to cultivate because the product concept is familiar, and the main marketing task is to communicate the benefits of the innovation to the target market. At the other end of the spectrum new product innovation may replicate a product that is already available. Innovators bear heavy development costs. Later entrants to the market may benefit from their innovation, and copy a product, but perhaps offer the product at a lower price and thereby gain a foothold in an existing market. Both of these last two approaches could be described as reactive, where an organization responds to a competitor's innovation and allows others to lead in establishing the market for the core concept, and then seeks a position in that market.

New product development requires a significant planning process, the length of which is highly dependent on the product and the specific marketplace. The process starts with idea generation. Ideas may emerge from research and development activities, competitors' activities or dialogue with customers, employees or partners. They should be screened in order to assess whether they can be developed to be consistent with the strategic plans and directions of the organization. Once the idea has been accepted in principle, concept testing can be used to test the idea with potential customers. Drawings, storyboards and mock-ups are used to describe, profile and visualize the product so that the reaction of a group of potential customers can be assessed. The next stage, business analysis, involves the development of production, marketing and financial projections. Product development involves product design and the development of production processes so that the product can actually be made. One of the first outcomes of this stage will be products that can be used in product testing and the next stage, test marketing. The purpose of test marketing is to indicate whether the target market will actually buy the product, and whether they are likely to be converted into loyal customers. Commercialization and product launch is the next stage. Finally, to complete the cycle, and to provide input to the next round of product innovation, attention needs to be paid to monitoring and evaluation. These stages of the new product development cycle are summarized in Figure 5.6. Two key points emerge from this consideration of the process:

1. New product development is complex.
2. New product development starts with consideration of markets, involves consideration of business processes, and revisits the marketplace for its reaction, before launch.

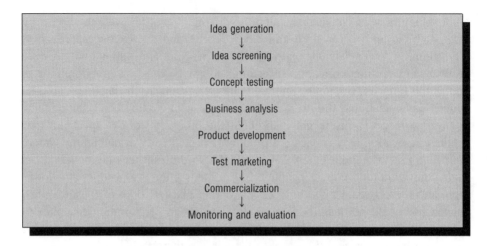

Idea generation
↓
Idea screening
↓
Concept testing
↓
Business analysis
↓
Product development
↓
Test marketing
↓
Commercialization
↓
Monitoring and evaluation

**Figure 5.6** The new product development process

## CONCLUSION

There is a wide range of information products, including elements of goods, services and information. An information product is one in which information is the core product. Products are continually redefined in interaction with customers. In the context of information, we have seen that it has a number of unique features that translate in different ways into information products. We then introduced the product lifecycle, which is useful for assessing marketing options. Organizations operate with product portfolios, which are dynamic and need to be managed. Product modification and innovation is an important element of product management.

## REFERENCES AND FURTHER READING

Adcock, D., Bradfield, R., Halborg, A. and Ross, C. (1998), *Marketing Principles and Practice*. 3rd edition. London: Pitman Publishing.

Baudrillard, J. (1988), *Jean Baudrillard: Selected Writings*, ed. M. Poster. Cambridge: Polity Press.

Dibb, S., Simkin, L., Pride, W.M. and Ferrell, O.C. (1994), *Marketing Concepts and Strategies*. 2nd European edition. Boston and London: Houghton Mifflin.

Eaton, J.J. and Bawden, D. (1991), 'What kind of resource is information?', *International Journal of Information Management*, **11**, 156–65.

Freiden, J., Goldsmith, R., Takacs, S. and Hofacker, C. (1998), 'Information as a product: not goods, not services', *Marketing Intelligence and Planning,* **16** (3), 1–13.

Garvin, D.A. (1984), 'Product quality: an important strategic weapon', *Business Horizons,* **27**, May–June, 40–43.

Mercer, D. (1996), *Marketing.* 2nd edition. Cambridge, MA: Blackwell.

Meyer, M.H. and Zack, M.H. (1996), 'The design and development of information products', *Sloan Management Review,* Spring, 43–59.

Mick, D.G. and Buhl, C. (1992), 'A meaning based model of advertising experiences', *Journal of Consumer Research,* **19**, 317–38.

Parasuraman, A., Zeithaml, V. and Berry, L. (1985), 'A conceptual model of service quality and its implications for future research', *Journal of Marketing,* **49** (Fall), 41–50.

Rowley, J.E. (1998), 'What is information?', *Information Services and Use,* **18** (4), 243–54.

Saren, M. and Tzokas, N. (1998), 'The nature of the product in market relationships', *Journal of Marketing Management,* **14** (5), 445–64.

Selnes, F. (1993), 'An examination of the effect of product performance on brand reputation, satisfaction and loyalty', *European Journal of Marketing,* **27** (9), 19–35.

Tapscott, D. (1996), *The Digital Economy.* New York: McGraw-Hill.

Usher, M.J. (1984), *Information Theory for Information Technologists.* London: Macmillan.

Webster, F.E. (1994), *Market-driven Management.* New York: Wiley.

# 6 Branding and corporate identity

## AIMS

Branding allows producers to differentiate their product from that of their competitors, and assists customers in the selection of an appropriate product. Branding is concerned with the creation of images and expectations in the minds of the consumer. These expectations may have a significant effect on the product or service selection and, in the case of services, the development of the service interaction. This chapter:

- defines some basic concepts associated with brands, branding and corporate identity;
- explores the benefits and disadvantages of branding; and
- outlines the stages in the process for the creation of a brand and corporate identity.

## INTRODUCTION

We are all aware of some of the well-known brands and brand names, such as Levi, Heinz, Cadbury's, Ford, Disney and Rolls-Royce. Such brand names are often taken by customers or potential customers as an indication of quality and expertise in a specific product range, and assist in the selection of a particular good or service. Branding allows producers to differentiate their product from that of their competitors and assists customers in their selection of an appropriate product. Branding is thus an essential extension of a product: it creates a character for a product that can be recognized in consumer markets. Although these concepts originated in the commercial world and, in that context, were originally associated primarily with goods rather than services, services are increasingly seeking to differentiate themselves from competitors through effective branding. Both public and private sector services have developed an increased awareness of the importance of marketing in the creation of effective communication with customers and potential customers. At a basic level, branding ensures that customers can immediately recognize the originator of the communication. Users should be able, through the use of elements of brand and design, to recognize a library's communications and identify positively with the brand. The creation of a brand is an important element of the promotional process, and is central to the use of promotion to convey a consistent message to customers about the nature of the organization and its products.

Kotler's (1994, p. 444) definition of a brand is a useful starting-point:

> A **brand** is a name, term, sign, symbol or design, or a combination of them, intended to identify the goods or services of one seller or group of sellers and to differentiate them from those of the competitors.

A brand can be viewed as the seller's promise consistently to deliver a specific set of benefits and services to the buyers. The brand enables the purchaser to obtain products that satisfy highly specific wants, without having to resort to a detailed description of them. As a shorthand expression, then, a brand facilitates the communication process between producer and customers. This expression may take the form of a name, term, design, symbol or any other feature that identifies one seller's good or service as distinct from those of other sellers. Typically, a brand may have one or more of the elements summarized in Figure 6.1: a brand name, a brandmark, a trademark, or a trade name.

*REFLECT: Examine a professional information magazine or a programme for a major conference and exhibition, and list some of the brand names used. Do they also have associated trademarks or brand marks?*

- A **brand name** is that part of a brand that can be spoken, including letters, words and numbers. A brand name is a significant identifier of products, e.g. 7-Up, Coca Cola.
- A **brand mark** is that element of a brand that is not made up of words – often a symbol or design – such as the symbols used to denote many car brands, the yellow arches of McDonalds and the Microsoft Windows symbol. These can also be registered as trademarks.
- A **trademark** is a legal designation in the form of a brand name, symbol or logo that is registered and protected for the owner's sole use. Organizations can register small sounds, product shapes and packaging as well as brand names and logos. Examples are: the shape of the Toblerone bar; the Nike symbol; and the Jif lemon juice packaging.
- A **trade name** is the full and legal name of an organization, e.g. Lever Brothers, Cadbury's. A trade name may or may not play a role in brand identification.

**Figure 6.1**  Elements of brand identifiers

# THE MEANING OF BRANDING

The simple definition of a brand given above belies the significance of the role of branding in consumer marketplaces. Branding is at the interface between product design, customer relationships and marketing communication. De Chernatony and Dall'Olmo Riley (1998) drew together twelve different definitions of brand, as shown in Figure 6.2. The first five definitions are covered by the basic definition of brand, but the next seven emphasize the role of brands in defining relationships with customers. The purpose of branding is to facilitate the organization's task of obtaining and maintaining a loyal customer base. In this context, the key definition is that of brand as an expression of a relationship between the consumer and the product. Indeed, many of the other definitions could be viewed as supporting the relationship between the brand and the customer. Thus logo and company are concerned with the first stage of relationship-building – awareness and recognition. Shorthand, identity and image are perhaps characteristic of the courting phase in a relationship, where a brand needs to make the first move. Risk reducer is concerned with facilitation of the early stages of a

| Brand definition | Brief explanation |
|---|---|
| Legal instrument | Mark of ownership as in trademark, name, or logo |
| Logo | Recognized name, term, design, symbol |
| Company | Recognizable corporate name and image |
| Shorthand | Represents characteristics or values that are associated with the brand |
| Risk reducer | Brand as a contract with the consumer |
| Identity system | Holistic, consistent, integrated vision |
| Image | Image in consumer's mind is the brand reality |
| Value system | Brand values to match relevant consumer values |
| Personality | Brands as symbolic devices with personalities that users value beyond their functional utility |
| Relationship | Extension of brand personality; brand is an expression of the relationship between the consumer and product |
| Adding value | Added-value differentiates brands; it is the non-functional benefits that are offered in addition to functional benefits. Consumers imbue brand with subjective meaning that they value sufficiently to cause them to buy the brand |
| Evolving entity | Brand concept changes by stage of development of the brand |

**Figure 6.2** Alternative definitions of the brand construct

97

relationship, possibly associated with cognition. In the concepts identity system, image, value system, personality, relationship and adding value a two-way dynamic is introduced, in which the consumer inputs into the brand, and the brand is consumer centred. At this stage the brand managers will be seeking to generate an affective orientation towards or an affinity with the brand.

In summary, then, brands should be seen as much more important than just a symbol or a clever bit of design. They symbolize various desirable product characteristics such as quality, reliability and professional approach, and act as a platform for establishing and extending relationships with customer groups.

*REFLECT: For the information product brands that you have identified above, can you identify some personality traits that you associate with the brand?*

## APPROACHES TO BRANDING

There are a number of different approaches to branding. Branding may relate to individual products, or groups of products, or to the organization or company name, as summarized in Figure 6.3. Although service sector industries may on occasion seek to brand their products, in general, there is significant emphasis on branding the company or, in other words, creating a corporate identity and seeking to influence the corporate image. The creation of a corporate identity is thus one type of branding, which is likely to be particularly appropriate in the context of library and information services. It is useful to distinguish between the concepts corporate identity and corporate image, as follows:

- **Individual branding** – naming each product differently. A poor product does not affect others; may be good for multiple segments, e.g. Proctor and Gamble (Tide, Bold, Daz and Dreft)
- **Family branding** – all products branded with the same name, e.g. Microsoft, Heinz; sometimes includes the company name; useful when physical differentiation is difficult and markets are relatively small
- **Family line branding** – family branding for products within a specified line, e.g. Ajax
- **Company name branding**, e.g. British Airways, American Express – often used in service sector
- **Brand extension** – use of an existing brand name as part of a brand for an improved or new product
- **Brand licensing** – permitting approved manufacturers to use a trademark for a licence fee, e.g. Disney, Jaguar
- **Own-label brands** – initiated and owned by resellers (wholesalers or retailers); manufacturers not identified on the product. Attractions are more efficient promotion, higher gross margins and improved store images
- **Generic brands** – no branding, economy packaging

**Figure 6.3** Approaches to branding

- **Corporate identity** is how the company or organization sees itself in terms of achievements, values, mission and aspects of products such as product range, price and quality.
- **Corporate image** is how the customer, potential customer, or other target audience perceives the organization in respect of some or all of the above features.

Thus, for a library and information service, corporate identity might emerge from general professional concerns associated with public service, customer care, and accessibility to a wide range of different information sources in both electronic and print media. Corporate image, in the eyes of the customers, may at the worst be associated with shelves of dusty and dry books, inconvenient opening hours and the need for silence.

Image, then, together with the expectations that may colour customers' quality judgements, is shaped to a considerable extent by previous experiences of a specific service point or of the category of service in general, such as, in this case, in libraries. The challenge for managers and marketers is to align corporate identity with corporate image. This should start with an assessment of both identity and image, and the development of a vision of potential identities and images.

Another important aspect of brands and branding emerges from this discussion of identity and image. Specifically, brand is a concept in the mind of the customer. Managers and marketers may choose to try to promote a specific brand identity, but they cannot entirely control brand image.

## BRANDS IN THE INFORMATION MARKETPLACE

Branding is most commonly associated with high-profile international consumer brands. Only a few brands will achieve such consumer familiarity. Many others are established in specific market segments and with specific professional or consumer groups. Accordingly there are a number of such brands in the information marketplace. Organizations such as libraries may be concerned with brands from two different perspectives:

- the creation of a corporate identity for their own products and services; and
- the evaluation of branded products and services provided by others in the information marketplace in the selection of goods and services that support their activities with end-consumers.

The significant brands that have established themselves over the past twenty or more years in the information marketplace include:

- brands relating to the technological infrastructure in which information management and delivery operate, such as IBM, Microsoft, Epson, Motorola;
- brands relating to organizations offering services to libraries, for example TFPL, OCLC, British Library, Talis, BASIS, GEAC;
- brands relating to specific products and services, for example Inside Information, UnCover;
- brands relating to publishers and database providers, for example Silverplatter, Oxford University Press, Chadwyck Healey, INSPEC, MEDLINE, Elsevier;
- brands relating to online hosts, for example Dialog, DataStar, Questel-Orbit, Lexis-Nexis.

One of the challenging characteristics of branding in the information environment is that technology has driven rapid change. This means that organizations must continually update their image and identity, and develop the meaning of brand names, some of which have a considerably longer life than others. In addition, brand names must have international validity, since many organizations operate in international marketplaces. From the consumer perspective, any indicators of the quality or nature of a service are particularly valued in a rapidly changing marketplace, so brands may become even more important.

## BENEFITS OF A BRAND

The benefits of a brand fall into the two interrelated categories of benefits to sellers and benefits to buyers.

### SELLER BENEFITS

One of the primary advantages of a brand is that it can be used to differentiate a product or service from that of the competitors. Plotting some well-known bands on a positioning map allows differentiation and subsequent development of imperfect competition and thereby competitive advantage, so that brands can sustain a price premium because customers perceive added-value. In addition, brands can encourage repeat purchasing of the same or similar products. So, for instance, if customers have a good experience with one product that they associate with a brand, they are likely to seek other products with the same brand, and expect the same quality, specification and value for money. Favourable experience with a brand is likely to lead to a degree of brand loyalty when customers consider repeat purchases. Any product that a customer needs to acquire or access on a regular basis, such as a visit to a library or a supermarket, depends significantly upon brand loyalty for return custom.

Another advantage of a brand is the opportunity for brand promotion, so that a series of products can be promoted simultaneously. One promotional campaign can thereby cover a range of products. So, for example, the brand 'Ford' may promote a range of cars, and although this range may change over time, the brand can remain consistent over a number of years. In the same way a publisher or a library and information service may seek to promote a collection of products under the one brand, for example Oxford University Press, Renfrewshire Library Services, GEAC Automation products.

## BUYER BENEFITS

Some of the benefits to the seller derive from the benefits to the buyer; we have touched on these above. It is useful, however, to reiterate that brands assist the customer with the purchase process. In particular, they help to reduce buyers' perceived risk of purchase and enable them to feel more confident in their purchase. This is largely because quality perceptions transfer from one branded product to another. A special case of this is prestige brands, such as Rolls-Royce, which are perceived to add status to the buyer in the eyes of their community, friends and family; customers are thus prepared to pay more for the name. So, for example, if a library has been successful in offering speedy interlibrary loan services, users might be more inclined to believe that the library might also be able to offer timely electronic access to business information.

*REFLECT: Identify one branded consumer product that you have purchased recently. What role did the brand play in your purchase decision?*

## DISADVANTAGES OF BRANDS

If brands lend support to both the buyer and the producer, why are there not many more strong brands? Part of the answer to this question lies in the limit to the number of brand images that individuals can retain, but there are also disadvantages to brands from the producer's perspective:

- Brands are expensive to establish; they need a great deal of promotion before the customer group recognizes a brand and associates specific attributes with it. Most successful brands have been built and maintained over a considerable period of time (often many years).
- Being associated too strongly with particular products or market positions can make it difficult for a producer to change the attributes of their product offering and to be associated with that change. So, for example, when Skoda sought to create a higher-quality product, which was more costly to produce

than the earlier models, they faced a real challenge in convincing the market that quality had increased to such an extent that they should consider paying higher prices for the product.

- Brands need to be maintained and protected. The brand image must be continually drawn to the attention of the customer.
- A brand may lead to differentiation and the opportunity to set higher prices, but calculating the asset value of a brand is difficult. But this must be done if a convincing case is to be made for investment in the creation and maintenance of a brand in a tight financial environment.

## CREATING A BRAND IMAGE OR CORPORATE IDENTITY

The creation of a brand image or a corporate identity must be prefaced by a consideration as to whether such branding is likely to be beneficial. This involves examination of the objectives of branding as identified below and an assessment of whether those objectives can realistically be achieved. It is important to recognize that some products will not benefit from branding, either because branding will not lend any advantage over competitors' products or because the nature of the product is such that a reputation will not assist users in their selection.

The process of brand creation is intimately associated with promotional activities; indeed, promotion is often a significant element of the process whereby a brand is created in the mind of the customers. Below we explore some aspects of this process, but first there are two other important considerations to take into account:

1. Brands are rarely created from a blank sheet. Most products or services have a prior brand image in the mind of the consumer, and this must be taken into account in developing any new image. Consistency and credibility are important in this process. The extent to which any prior brand needs to be taken into account depends upon the strength of its identity.
2. The brand identity needs to be carried through both internal and external communication, so if a specific form of name is chosen for an organization, for example Leisureforce, then this form must be used in both internal and external communication, and variants such as Leisure Force, Leisure force or LF must not be tolerated. Further the identity must be something that all staff can understand and translate into their role in the organization.

## ORGANIZATIONAL CONTEXT

Organizational context will determine which products, product lines or organizations are an appropriate focus for branding. Many library and information services may be concerned to create a brand for the service in its entirety, but, in so doing, may need to accommodate the corporate identity of the wider organization, such as the higher education institution, professional body, college or local authority of which they are part. There must be shared values across different parts of an organization, reflected in the brand image created at different levels in the organization.

## OBJECTIVES

What is the objective of the brand and the branding exercise? Typical aims of any promotion exercise can often be grouped into the following categories:

- to increase sales;
- to maintain or improve market share;
- to create a favourable climate for future sales;
- to inform and educate the market;
- to create a competitive difference;
- to improve promotional efficiency.

Branding might contribute to the achievement of any of these objectives, but it is important to decide where priorities should lie.

The identification and characteristics of the target audience are part of the objective-setting process. Is the brand message to be communicated to customers or potential customers? Is the message a 'mass' message or should it be focused on specific groups? How might those groups be defined or segmented?

The final stage in objective-setting is to consider the message. This must initially gain attention and subsequently hold the interest of the audience, and possibly lead to action in the form of purchase or use on their part.

## DESIGNING A BRAND NAME AND VISUAL IDENTITY

The brand name is an important component of the brand identity, and must create an immediate and lasting impression for the brand. Brand names should be:

- easy for customers to say, spell and recall, and, for the global marketplace, acceptable in different languages;
- appropriate for use as part of a URL, so that users can easily identify Websites in the electronic marketplace, for example Online Inc., Ovid;

- distinctive, and standing out from the competition whilst appealing to the target market and being appropriate to the product, for example Instant Library, Clearview, Context;
- compatible with all products in the line, for example Business Information Focus, Book Data;
- suitable for use in all types of media, for example Anbar, Proquest;
- capable of protection through registration, and not subject to becoming generic: descriptive brand names such as aspirin, Liquorice Allsorts or Weet-abix are particularly vulnerable to this;
- not subject to brand counterfeiting or copying;
- if possible and appropriate, indicative of major benefits. Names such as Ex-Lax, Brittany Ferries and Papermate convey application and benefits. Other examples might be Infomatch, OneSource, and Database Publishing Systems.

Normally the brand name will be incorporated into the visual identity, or the physical embodiment of the corporate identity. This visual identity normally also includes a colour, a typeface and possibly a logo. The physical embodiment of the corporate identity must be distinctive, usable, have immediate impact and be suitable for use in a variety of different contexts and media.

### COMMUNICATION CHANNELS

Communication channels include personal and non-personal channels. In the service sector personal communication channels are especially important. These fall into two groups: customer-to-customer communication channels and service agent-to-customer communication channels. Both of these categories are embedded in the service process: service experiences will influence images. Non-personal communication channels include the press, both local and national, brochures and pamphlets, television, the Internet and other public access information points, posters, radio and the cinema. Whilst a library will often be concerned to communicate primarily with a 'local' user community, it is likely to select those channels that provide targeted visibility to that community and are economical. Typically these might include literature, community information service points, local radio and posters. An important consideration in the selection of communication channels is the available budget.

### MONITORING BRAND CREATION

The effectiveness of any brand creation process or campaign should be evaluated, so that the use of resources can be monitored and so that the organization continues to have a sound understanding of its brand image in the minds of its customers upon which to base further promotion. Remember too, that, to avoid brands becoming dated, they must be changed and developed over a period of time, even if they retain certain core values, such as a commitment to quality.

## BRAND EXTENSION

If a brand has been created to cover specific products and marketplaces, as product ranges develop, or there is a need to move into new marketplaces, organizations might be keen to use the reputation and relationships associated with established brands in these different contexts. Using the same brand name for different products and audiences is described as brand extension. In the information marketplace, services and products can change relatively rapidly, when compared with the several years that it might typically take to establish a brand. Some organizations have created new brands for their e-commerce activities (for example, Egg, the e-banking arm of the Prudential), but most information providers see benefits in using the same brand in both print and electronic marketplaces. An important element of the maintenance of a brand is the consideration of brand extension, and the effect on the brand of a changing portfolio of products.

## CONCLUSION

This chapter has explored elements of the concepts of branding and the creation of a corporate identity. Although these concepts originated in the commercial world, and in that context were originally primarily associated with goods rather than services, services are increasingly seeking to differentiate themselves from competitors through effective branding. Both public and private sector services have developed an increased awareness of the importance of marketing in the creation of effective communication with customers and potential customers. The creation of a brand is an important element of the promotional process. Brands have a key role in conveying a consistent message to customers about the nature of the organization and its products. The benefits of branding include those for both seller and consumer, and in general outweigh the disadvantages. The main disadvantage of a brand is the possibility of being associated with outmoded images. The process associated with the creation of a brand image or corporate identity involves consideration of the objectives of branding and the context in which it is being undertaken. The design of the brand name and visual identity, and the selection of communication channels, are important elements in this process. Finally, the success of the brand creation should be monitored.

# REFERENCES

Adcock, D., Bradfield, R., Halborg, A. and Ross, C. (1998), *Marketing Principles and Practice*. 3rd edition. London: Pitman Publishing.

Arnold, D. (1992), *The Handbook of Brand Management*. London: Century Business, The Economist Books.

De Chernatony, L. and Dall'Olmo Riley, F. (1998), 'Defining a "Brand": beyond the literature with experts' interpretations', *Journal of Marketing Management*, **14** (5), 417–43.

De Chernatony, L. and McDonald, M. (1998), *Creating Powerful Brands in Consumer, Service and Industrial Markets*. 2nd edition. Oxford: Butterworth Heinemann.

Kapferer, J.-N. (1992), *Strategic Brand Management*. London: Kogan Page.

Kotler, P. (1994), *Marketing Management: Analysis, Planning, Implementation and Control*. 8th edition. London: Prentice Hall International.

Martinson, R. (1995), 'The role of brands in European marketing', *Journal of Brand Management*, **2** (4), 161–6.

Sharp, B.M. (1993), 'Managing brand extension', *Journal of Consumer Marketing*, **10** (3), 14–21.

Woodward, S. (1991), 'Competitive marketing', in *Understanding Brands by 10 People Who Do*, ed. D. Cowley. London: Kogan Page, pp. 119–34.

# 7 Marketing communications

## AIMS

Promotion is used to communicate with customers in connection with product offerings. It has a key role in determining profitability and market success and is one of the key '4Ps' of the marketing mix. This chapter explores:

- the promotional mix, including its tools, advertising campaigns and the use of advertising agencies;
- the stages in the design of communications strategies, including a discussion of concepts such as target audiences, marketing messages, communication channels, promotional budgets and monitoring promotional performances; and
- approaches to the use of key elements in the communications mix, including advertising, direct marketing, exhibitions, personal selling, public relations and sponsorship.

## INTRODUCTION

Promotion is used by organizations to communicate with customers in respect of their product offerings. In this sense, promotion is one side of the communication process with customers. Marketing research (Chapter 9), in which suppliers seek to elicit information on consumer requirements, complements promotion. Figure 7.1 depicts this very simply.

In some forms of promotion and service delivery, communication in both directions can be achieved simultaneously, and since two-way communication is the only real communication, these forms should be encouraged. Examples of two-way promotion emerge largely from the contexts of services marketing and relationship marketing. In the former, for example, promotion can be part of the service delivery.

**Figure 7.1**  Promotion and its complement, market research

Exchanges between the service agent and the customer can elicit information about customer requirements, and also enable the service agent to explain how the organization's products might meet them. Similar kinds of exchanges can occur in organizational marketing transactions, where the salesperson is a significant agent in the establishment of relationships between the customer and the organization. The use of loyalty and reward cards in, say, supermarkets is another approach that fulfils both promotional and market research aims.

Mercer (1996), in emphasizing that communication must be a two-way process, says:

> The ideal form of promotion is the conversation which takes place between the expert sales professional and his or her customer. It is interactive and conversation is specific to the needs of both. Other forms of promotion, which deal in the 'average' needs of groups of people can only hope to approximate to this ideal. (p. 309)

Nevertheless, as Mercer acknowledges, much promotion, especially in consumer markets, can appear to be predominantly a one-way process, in which the producer decides upon a marketing message and selects channels through which to communicate that message.

In such contexts, there is feedback on the effectiveness of the promotional strategy, but since this is largely in the form of sales, it can be difficult to differentiate between the role of promotion and the contribution of other factors in the marketing mix to market success.

The information marketplace is an interesting mixture of consumer and business-to-business marketing. For example, libraries are often concerned to promote services to end-users or consumers, and increasingly online search services and other Web search services are seeking to capture the end-user market. At the same time, library suppliers, online search services, database producers and publishers of journals and abstracting and indexing services have often viewed their primary market to be other organizations, such as libraries, businesses and public sector organizations.

This chapter first explores the promotional mix and the role of promotion. It then emphasizes the need to take a systematic approach to promotion, and discusses this in the context of advertising campaigns. The stages in designing communication strategies are outlined. Finally, the characteristics of specific elements in the promotional mix are described.

## THE PROMOTIONAL MIX

Promotion is one of the key 4Ps in the marketing mix (Dibb et al., 1994) and as such has an important role to play in market success. Promotion is concerned with ensuring that customers are aware of the products that the organization makes available to them. More specifically, the objectives of any promotional strategy will be drawn from an appropriate mixture of the following roles of promotion:

1. To increase sales
2. To maintain or improve market share
3. To create or improve brand recognition
4. To create a favourable climate for future sales
5. To inform and educate the market
6. To create a competitive advantage relative to competitors' products or market position
7. To improve promotional efficiency.

*REFLECT: Rewrite the above objectives in terms that apply to a library seeking to promote its services to its users.*

An appropriate promotional mix must be created in order to meet the objectives of any given promotion strategy. This mix is the combination of different channels used to communicate a promotional message. Selection is made from the range of tools that are available as part of the promotional mix, including:

- **Advertising**, which includes any paid form of non-personal presentation and promotion of ideas, goods or services by any identified sponsor. The pages of professional newsletters and magazines are common avenues for advertising information products.
- **Direct marketing**, which includes the use of mail, telephone or other non-personal contact tools to communicate with or solicit a response from specific customers and prospects. Mail shots and leaflets inserted in professional magazines are used to promote information products.
- **Sales promotion**, which includes short term incentives to encourage trial or purchase of a product or service, such as discounts for access to a database over a limited period.
- **Public relations and publicity**, which includes programmes designed to

promote and/or protect a company's image, or that of its products, including product literature, exhibitions and articles about organizations' products in professional or in-house newsletters.

- **Personal selling**, which includes face-to-face interaction with one or more prospective purchasers for the purpose of making sales. This is common within the organizational marketing transactions in the information industry, where sales representatives, often also with a support function, are the norm.
- **Sponsorship**, which includes financial or external support of an event or person by an unrelated organization or donor, such as is common in the arts, sports and charities. Large organizations, such as major publishing groups like Reed Elsevier, or software houses such as Microsoft, may engage in sponsorship, but in education and libraries, public sector organizations are more likely to be the recipients of sponsorship.

Typically, organizations will use a combination of these strategies; indeed, one promotional strategy may be used to support another promotional event. For example, an organization might take out a newspaper advertisement to announce its sponsorship of a sporting event. All elements of the marketing mix must be integrated, so that together they communicate and reinforce the message. Marketing communications initiatives for specific products may have a product-specific message, and indeed some media may permit more elaboration on the message than others, but all these variations on the message must be elements in an integrated communications strategy.

The choice of elements in the promotional mix is determined by:

- the nature of the product and, specifically, how much personal support is needed in the decision-making process associated with the choice of the product, and other factors that determine the need to establish a relationship between the customer and the provider. In many information environments, the user needs support and training in the use of products, and in service contexts a relationship is important in encouraging repeat visits and continued patronage;
- the target audience for the communication, and the medium through which they can most easily be reached;
- the lifecycle stage of a service or product. Promotion for new products is concerned with raising awareness; later in the lifecycle, sustaining relationships and fending off competition might require different media channels;
- the marketplace situation and, in particular, the degree and nature of the competition and the promotional channels used by competitors;
- the available budget!

## ADVERTISING CAMPAIGNS

An integrated marketing communications package is not achieved through a series of random promotional initiatives. Organizations that seek to communicate with large consumer audiences plan and execute advertising campaigns. These ensure that a common theme is communicated through a series of messages placed in selected media, chosen for their expected cumulative impact on the target audiences. Such campaigns may run for varying lengths of time. Some organizations run them on an annual basis, such as a drink-and-driving campaign that might be run each Christmas. Libraries might run such campaigns for National Book Week; academic libraries might do so at around enrolment periods to heighten awareness of new students to library resources. Typically such annual campaigns have a common theme, but the theme needs to be communicated in different ways in each year. The stages in an advertising campaign parallel those described below as the stages in the design and implementation of communication strategies.

A key issue in the planning and execution of an advertising campaign is allocation of the responsibility for it. There are three options:

1. An individual with functional or product or service responsibility
2. The organization's marketing department
3. An external advertising agency.

Libraries do not in general have their own marketing departments, and so the responsibility may often lie with a library manager, who also has a range of other responsibilities in respect of the library service. On the other hand, many libraries exist within organizations that do have marketing departments, and it is important to work with these, as they can offer a range of expertise and contacts who may assist in any library-specific promotion activities. In addition, any promotional activities associated with a library or information service must take into account corporate marketing messages being disseminated through the organization's marketing department. Other organizations in the information industry may have specialized marketing departments. Many such departments use advertising agencies to support the design and implementation of a marketing campaign.

## DESIGNING COMMUNICATIONS STRATEGIES

Figure 7.2 summarizes the stages in the design of communications strategies to support the realization of promotional objectives. In the launch of a new, re-

- Identify target audience
- Determine communication objectives
- Design the message
- Select communication channels
- Establish promotional budget
- Decide on promotional mix
- Evaluation

**Figure 7.2** Stages in designing communication strategies

designed or rebranded product these stages would form the steps in the planning of a promotional campaign. However, many organizations are not only concerned with specific promotional campaigns, but also with maintaining a continued awareness and positive attitude to their products. In such circumstances, whilst each of these stages remains important, they will not necessarily always be visited in the sequence shown in the figure. In the next few sections, the purpose of each stage is described in further detail.

## IDENTIFICATION OF TARGET AUDIENCE

The first stage is to characterize the **target audience**. This audience may include the complete market segment for the product or the organization, or a specific promotional strategy may be targeted more narrowly at a niche within the broader segment. Messages and channels may be selected accordingly, but care must be taken to ensure that other groups in the market segment are not alienated by the messages that might be associated with a niche strategy. The characteristics of the audience need to be understood. Segmentation might be applicable here, but in addition it will be important to understand the types of marketing messages to which the audience is likely to be susceptible (for example, is convenience or price a priority?) and to be aware of the audience's current image of the company and its products. The concept of brands and brand image was explored in Chapter 6.

## DETERMINING COMMUNICATION OBJECTIVES

Below the level of the **objectives** of the promotional strategy, are the objectives of the communication strategy. How these can be categorized depends on the model of the communication or promotional process that is regarded as appropriate. Figure 7.3 compares four different models of this communication process. Each can be identified as having three stages:

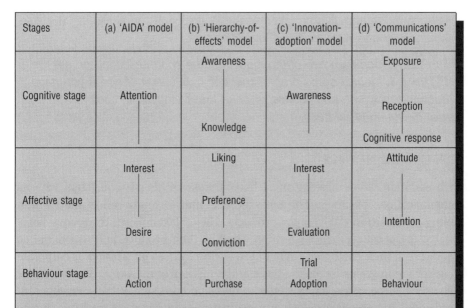

| Stages | (a) 'AIDA' model | (b) 'Hierarchy-of-effects' model | (c) 'Innovation-adoption' model | (d) 'Communications' model |
|---|---|---|---|---|
| Cognitive stage | Attention | Awareness<br><br>Knowledge | Awareness | Exposure<br><br>Reception<br><br>Cognitive response |
| Affective stage | Interest<br><br>Desire | Liking<br>Preference<br>Conviction | Interest<br><br>Evaluation | Attitude<br><br>Intention |
| Behaviour stage | Action | Purchase | Trial<br>Adoption | Behaviour |

*Sources*: (a) F.K. Strong, *The Psychology of Selling* (New York: McGraw-Hill, 1925), p. 9; (b) Robert J. Lavidge and Gary A. Steiner, 'A model for predictive measurements of advertising effectiveness', *Journal of Marketing*, October 1961, p. 61; (c) Everett M. Rogers, *Diffusion of Innovations* (New York: Free Press, 1962), pp. 79–86; (d) various sources.

**Figure 7.3**  Models of marketing communication

1. The **cognitive** stage, during which potential customers become aware of products
2. The **affective** stage, during which customers form opinions and attitudes concerning products
3. The **behaviour** stage, during which customers take action (such as making a purchase) on the basis of their experiences in the first two stages.

Arguably the best known of these models is the AIDA model. This includes the following four elements:

- Attention – when the customer becomes aware of the product
- Interest – when an interest in the product develops
- Desire – when the customer has developed a sense of wanting the product
- Action – when a purchase is made.

It is important to decide whether the objective is to draw to attention, cultivate interest, stimulate desire or provoke action. In formulating communication objectives, account should also be taken of the structure of the consumer decision-making process, as discussed in Chapter 3.

> REFLECT: Compare two of the models of the communication process in Figure 7.3. Identify some promotional communication of which you have been the recipient, and assess which of these stages the communication was designed to address.

## DESIGNING THE MESSAGE

Each communication strategy must have a message that is consistent with its communication objectives. The message will often strongly reflect the **unique selling proposition** (USP) of the products. The USP comprises the unique benefits that the producer believes are provided by their product, and which will be of interest to their customers. Where promotion focuses on a brand or corporate image or identity, this forms the basis of the marketing message. Another factor that needs to be taken into account is message consistency between different campaigns. An organization should promote a consistent, if evolving, image through all its separate campaigns; otherwise the audience will become confused and no overall clear message will be communicated.

The elements of the message that need to be considered are:

- message content – what message to communicate (e.g., 'We are offering free public access Web services');
- message structure – how to express the message (e.g., 'Want to learn how to browse the Web for free?');
- message format – how to represent the message in symbols (e.g., whether to include pictures, more complete text details, embedding the message in catalogues, posters, presentations);
- message source – who should communicate the message, or act as the spokesperson, either in person, or by signature; the options are other customers, significant public figures, or the service agent (e.g., 'Would you like to try our new Web service?').

Examples of potential message content for library and information services are given in Figure 7.4.

## SELECTING COMMUNICATION CHANNELS

Communication channels can be divided into personal and non-personal. The former are those in which two or more people communicate with one another, and **word of mouth** is the primary means of communication, although other

**Books for Babies** – an initiative to encourage parents to teach their children to learn from books at a very early age.

*Messages*:

- Learning can start early
- Introducing your baby to books is fun
- Your baby will enjoy books
- Your local public library can provide access to a good range of books for babies
- Babies are welcome in the library

**Southport's History in Pictures** – an exhibition to promote the use of the public library's local history collection

*Messages*:

- See Southport one hundred years ago
- How has Southport changed?
- Enjoy remembering
- Find out about your heritage
- Discover life in Southport as it was

**Studying with Electronic Journals** – a series of training events to encourage students to develop the use of e-journals in the course of their studies

*Messages*:

- E-journals are an important resource for your dissertation
- Training makes your study more efficient and effective, freeing time for other activities
- Get better grades
- Impress your tutor
- Avoid the queues for print resources
- Study at home

**E-Commerce Alert** – a new Web-based current-awareness service announcing e-commerce developments from the Chartered Institute of Marketing (a professional body) to their members on a subscription basis

*Messages*:

- Keep up to date with e-commerce developments
- Keep one step ahead of your competitors in the e-marketplace
- Easy-to-read profiles, digests and links to Websites demonstrating innovations

**Figure 7.4** Examples of potential message content for library and information services

media, such as e-mail, are growing in significance. There are three types of personal communication channels:

1. Advocate channels, such as company salespeople
2. Expert channels, such as independent experts, including software and CD-ROM reviewers

3. Social channels and consultants, such as friends, professional colleagues and professional networks.

Exhibitions are an important arena in which advocate channels, such as sales-people, can come into contact with customers. These are widely used in promotion to organizations. In this context personal conversation will be supplemented, for example by leaflets, posters, videos and samples (such as sample discs).

Non-personal communication channels are those in which communication is through some other medium other than person to person. These include:

1. **The Press**, including national and regional newspapers and magazines, but most significantly for the information industry, trade, professional and technical journals
2. **Television**, including satellite, cable and digital television. The expensive nature of this medium means that it is only an option for major advertisers
3. **Radio** offers a wide range of competitively priced promotional options. In general it is deemed to have less potential impact than television since there is no visual image
4. **Posters** can be placed in a wide variety of different environments, from billboards at the roadside to the underground and other public places, such as libraries and notice boards within organizations
5. **Leaflets and publicity** are important 'takeaways' that can act as reminders of products and contact points
6. **The Web** is important when users are likely to be operating in a virtual world. Most organizations have a Web page, but the extent to which they use this for commerce and community-building varies.

## ESTABLISHING THE BUDGET

The available budget has a significant effect on the range of communication activities that can be pursued. For many libraries marketing budgets are extremely limited, but commercial organizations in the information marketplace have marketing budgets that are consistent with (if not sufficient for!) the market segments with which they need to establish and maintain communications. This chapter seeks to embrace both ends of this spectrum by reviewing the full range of options, whilst also identifying options that are relatively low cost. As will be discussed later, some channels in the promotional mix are inherently more expensive than others, and some incur only hidden costs, such as those associated with staff time. Managers must be aware of the costs of communication activities, even when they do not generate a separate invoice, and should continually monitor the value and impact associated with marketing communications activities.

Where formal marketing budgets are available, most are a compromise! The basis for the calculation of a promotional budget is one or more of:

1. The resource that can be made available for marketing
2. A percentage of sales (say, 5 per cent)
3. The budget necessary to seek to achieve 'share-of-voice' parity with competitors (for example, if a competitor has a regular advertisement in a local newspaper, it *might* be advisable to seek the same level of exposure)
4. The budget necessary to meet the desired objectives, taking into account the required activities (known as objective task or activity budgeting).

The last of these approaches is the most rational, but there are constraints on all budgets, and affordability is often a prime consideration.

## DECIDING ON THE PROMOTIONAL MIX

The promotional mix will normally include a selection of strategies from more than one of the following: advertising; direct marketing; sales promotion; public relations and publicity; personal selling; and sponsorship. The factors that should be considered in establishing an appropriate promotional mix include:

- The available budget
- The marketing message
- The complexity of the product or service
- Market size and location
- Distribution of the product
- The stage in the product lifecycle
- Competition.

To return specifically to the issue of the distribution of the product, promotional activities can focus directly on end-users or may, alternatively, be directed to intermediaries in the distribution channel, as shown in Figure 7.5. Promotional activities to intermediaries such as libraries, teachers and lecturers are described as push strategies, and rely upon intermediaries 'selling' the product to the end-user. Direct promotion to end-users is designed to encourage them to ask for certain features or products so that intermediaries experience a demand to which they would be wise to respond.

In particular, the decision to use a pull or a push strategy determines whether promotion is focused on organizational marketing or on end-user/consumer

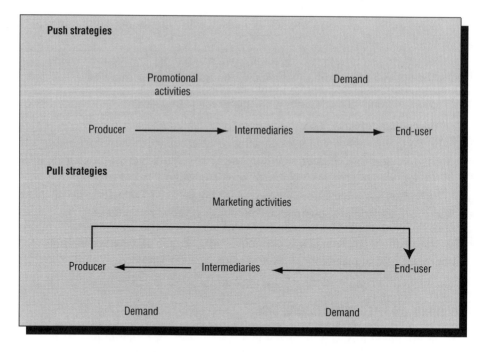

**Figure 7.5** Pull and push promotional strategies

marketing; the appropriate communication channels in these two markets are very different.

The media plan should be one by-product of this selection of communications media. This should specify the exact media and times and dates of appearance of advertisements.

## MEASURING PROMOTION RESULTS

Promotion incurs considerable investment. It can frequently be difficult to differentiate between the effect of promotion and the other elements of the marketing mix. Nevertheless, it is important to monitor the effects of promotion by looking at sales figures and any measures of reputation that are available.

## PUBLIC RELATIONS

Organizations cannot function effectively without the support and cooperation of financial backers, employees, trade unions, suppliers, legal and regulatory bodies to which they are answerable, interested pressure groups, and the media.

There is no direct trading relationship between the organization and many of these 'publics'. In communicating with them the organization must focus on explaining what it stands for, and creating a strong positive corporate image. Public relations (PR) deals with the quality and nature of the relationship between an organization and its publics. Its objective is to generate communication, thereby influencing attitudes and opinions, and to achieve mutual understanding. PR may be concerned with activities such as:

- the creation and maintenance of a corporate identity and image;
- the enhancement of the organization's standing in the community;
- the communication of the organization's philosophy and purpose;
- relationships with the media;
- attendance at trade exhibitions.

PR then, comprises press releases and other relationships with the media, events, publications, lobbying, house journals and newsletters, and briefings.

PR has the following positive characteristics when compared with advertising:

- **Credibility** – editorial comment carries more authority and credibility; readers expect advertisements to be partisan.
- **Reach** – PR may reach wider or different audiences, including managers, community leaders and other stakeholders, who may or may not be users or customers. PR can lend sponsors good publicity, and leave a positive image with others who have influence in political and financial arenas.
- **Cost** – no advertising costs are incurred, although PR is not free. Effective PR requires commitment to and resources for a planned programme.
- **Excitement** – PR is, by definition, news, and must be written so that it attracts readers' interest.

The major disadvantage of PR is that it is uncontrollable. Editors control what is published, and it is not always the case that all publicity is good publicity!

Publicity and relationships with the media are a major component of PR. A primary tool for communicating with the media is the press release, but an integral element of PR is the building of relationships with editorial staff of newspapers (often regional and local newspapers), trade and professional magazines, and radio and television. The two sets of practical tips (Figures 7.6 and 7.7) give an insight into some key issues for managing and organizing PR, and creating a press release, respectively.

- PR channels must be selected to reach the target audience. An awareness of the media channels used by target audiences is a prerequisite for effective PR.
- Details of potential media channels, such as the name and address of the editor, copy date for issues or programmes, and profile of readers, listeners or viewers, can be gleaned from a media pack.
- Cultivate a relationship with specific media by trying to understand the type of copy that an editor is seeking. Specifically:
  - note any upcoming theme issues and offer to contribute in advance
  - focus on news
  - offer human-interest stories, such as local student success or conference presentations by a manager
  - organize events
  - talk to editors and get feedback on the items that have been submitted

**Figure 7.6**  Practical tips on developing a PR strategy

- Use clear headings to indicate that it is a press release; give the originator
- Include date
- Give the piece a title
- Use double-spaced text
- Summarize the whole item in the first paragraph, which can be scanned quickly
- Use subsequent paragraphs to describe clearly the event, product or service
- Use jargon-free language
- Give contact details for readers, including a Website address
- Give contact details for follow-up calls from the press

**Figure 7.7**  Practical tips on content and format for a press release

## ADVERTISING

Advertising can be defined as any paid form of non-personal promotion transmitted through a mass medium. The sponsor should be clearly identified, and the advertisement may relate to an organization, a product or a service. There are two types of advertising: product and institutional, and it is useful to differentiate between the typical objectives of these two types, even though there is reinforcement between them.

*REFLECT: Which of the objectives identified in Figure 7.8 are being achieved through an academic library Website that offers pointers to a collection of Web-based subject resources?*

Advertising has until recently been an anathema to public sector organizations, and the absence of identifiable marketing budgets has acted as a significant

| Objectives of product advertising | Objectives of institutional advertising |
|---|---|
| • Explain a new product<br>• Emphasize unique benefits<br>• Compare with competition<br>• Remind customers about a product<br>• Reinforce customers' perceptions of benefits<br>• Encourage repeat purchase or engagement with the service | • Disseminate information on new developments<br>• Reinforce the organization's image<br>• Create and maintain the character of the organization<br>• Communicate a view on an issue |

**Figure 7.8** Comparing the objectives of product and institutional advertising

barrier to its use. However, with the marketization of the public sector, many library and information services are exploring the potential of advertising for communicating with specific audiences. Although advertising in the 'mass media' is expensive, advertising in local and regional newspapers, general and special interest trade and professional magazines, and the use of billboards and notice-boards offers cost-effective avenues for communicating with niche audiences. In addition, although payment is inherent in the definition of advertising, in-house newsletters, electronic noticeboards, and Websites are opportunities for free advertising. Some of these channels may also be particularly useful for communicating messages to staff in large organizations.

One form of advertising that all organizations engage in from time to time is that associated with staff recruitment. Typically these advertisements are placed by personnel departments, and will be presented in the corporate style. They offer an opportunity to communicate with a different target audience to that which might be reached through other channels. For secretarial, administrative and assistant posts, such advertisements are an opportunity for visibility in the local and regional press. For professional posts, they will be visible to the professional community, who may be significant opinion-formers in a wider marketplace.

*REFLECT: List all the media in which your information service might usefully place advertisements. Describe the target audience that those advertisements would be designed to reach.*

Advertising reaches communities and individuals beyond those with whom the organization already has a relationship, or with whom direct contact is difficult or expensive. Examples of situations in which advertising is useful include:

• where there are large target audiences (such as those associated with public libraries);
• when the name of the most appropriate contact in an organization is unknown;

- when libraries need to widen their marketplace, perhaps for one particular service or product, for example a subject gateway, or public access to the Internet.

In these contexts advertising is good for:

- communicating simple messages, such as announcing the launch of a new service, an open evening, or extended opening hours;
- establishing and reinforcing brand image and loyalty, through bringing the product or organization to the audience's attention;
- visibility in the marketplace, especially if competitors do not advertise;
- selling specific items, such as a search service, a publication, or a CD-ROM.

Most advertisements in the information marketplace are placed in magazines and newspapers. Although such media are less glamorous than broadcast media, they have powerful advantages. With such media, people have selected what they want to read, have an interest which they are actively pursuing, and thus pay attention and absorb what they read. Print media are also often circulated to other readers, and may be retained for later reference. Practical tips for creating good print advertisements are given in Figure 7.9. Examples of recent marketing messages in the information marketplace are shown in Figure 7.10.

## DIRECT MARKETING

Direct marketing is an interactive system of marketing which uses one or more advertising medium to effect a measurable response at any location, forming a basis for creating and further developing an ongoing direct relationship between an organization and its customers. Key aspects of this definition are that direct marketing is:

- personalized and targeted, and normally addressed to named individuals. The

- Create a heading to catch the eye with informative or emotional appeal
- Follow the headline with limited and carefully phrased body text
- Use illustrations effectively – these are sometimes more important than the text
- Sell the benefits
- Communicate to the individual, and show an understanding of the target audience
- Be credible – avoid clichés and oversell
- Keep the message and style simple, clear and concise
- Offer contact points, including names
- Pay attention to design and layout

**Figure 7.9**  **Practical tips on good print advertisements**

| Organization | Product | Message |
|---|---|---|
| Dialog Corporation | Online databases | It's online |
| OCLC | Online search service, electronic collection services | Complete, customized library solutions, not just databases |
| ISI | Current Contents Connect, Web of Science | We don't plan the future, but we plan to be part of it |
| Encyclopedia Britannica International Ltd | Britannica Online | *What.can.you.get.@britannica.online* |
| Ovid | Full-text electronic journals and bibliographic databases | Aggregated. Integrated. 100% searchable electronic full text from Ovid |
| EDINA | Subject gateway | Working in partnership to bring networked resources to higher education |
| H.W. Wilson | Abstract and full-text databases | Wilson Full Text – now available in the format you need: Web, Windows, Mac, DOS, or magnetic tape |
| Catchword | Electronic publishing software | Realpage: the electronic publishing solution from Catchword |
| Northern Light | Search engine | You're a corporate librarian. Obviously you're in it for the glory |
| Reed Elsevier | CD-ROMs, databases, electronic journals, ScienceDirect | Information provider to the world |
| MINTEL | Marketing intelligence | Bringing consumer research into focus |
| Questel-Orbit | Online search services | In a sea of information every droplet counts |

**Figure 7.10**  Examples of recent messages in advertisements in the information marketplace

targeting inherent in direct mail means that it can communicate more focused and complex messages than can be carried in advertising;

- interactive, in that a response is requested from the recipient. This response must be identifiable and measurable. This makes it easy to measure the impact of direct mail;
- part of the establishment of a relationship between the organization and its customers. A series of positive experiences or interactions can increase customer confidence and loyalty.

In addition, direct mail, one of the main avenues for direct marketing, is flexible in terms of what can be included in the package: CDs, videos, gift and samples all add a further dimension to the communication experience. Other offers, such as free exhibition tickets, or an invitation to a reception to celebrate the opening of a new building, or an invitation to be one of the first participants in a pilot trial of a new alerting service, may be used to prompt a response.

The success of direct marketing depends on careful targeting and branding. To be able to create and sustain quality relationships with many individual customers, an organization needs to know as much as possible about each customer, and must be able to access, manipulate and analyse this information. An effective database is central to building effective relationships and knowing customers. Unfortunately, creating and maintaining a database of appropriate contacts can be time-consuming. In the library context, the database should include people from all of the various stakeholder groups. Some details of registered library users may be available from the registration or borrower database. An interesting subgroup might be lapsed users. Other contact names and details may be drawn from correspondence, internal telephone directories, intranet membership lists, newsletters, trade directories, yearbooks, and press and professional contacts. The electoral roll and mailing lists that can be purchased from suppliers of such lists may be useful in some circumstances. As information providers increasingly interact with their users through electronic means, it will be possible to collect contact addresses from these communications. Typical details in a database might include:

- Name
- Job title
- Department
- Address
- Telephone
- Fax
- e-mail
- Website address
- Nature of organization
- Market sector
- Interests.

These data would support contact (for direct mail or other purposes) by mail, telephone, fax or e-mail. Individuals could, for example, be selected from this list on the basis of their job title, Website address, geographical location, market sector or interests. The relationship between a database to support promotional activities and the data that are gathered about customers through market research and marketing information systems should be considered. There may be differences between the coverage of the two types of database and the data that need to be collected for the different purposes. Nevertheless, an **integrated marketing database** that supports both functions will reduce the time involved in database maintenance, and should improve the quality of the database.

*REFLECT: What sources could your organization easily access to support the development of a database for use in direct marketing?*

In addition to direct mail, two other forms of direct marketing are direct response advertising and telemarketing. The first of these is associated with the placing of advertisements that carry a response section; its completion and return provide the data to create a marketing database of the respondents. Telemarketing using the telephone is a direct, personal approach. It is a planned and controlled activity that creates and exploits a direct relationship between the customer and the seller. Many customers find telemarketing intrusive, because they feel forced into a dialogue. Used sensitively, it may, however, have application in marketing communication and service evaluation.

*REFLECT: In what circumstances would you find it acceptable to be contacted by an information service provider and be prepared to discuss their services?*

## SALES PROMOTIONS

The aim of sale promotions is to add extra value to a product, service or experience over and above the normal product offering, so as to create an extra inducement for customers to buy or try it. Although individual sales promotions are usually short-term tactical measures, sales promotion is an important strategic element in the promotional mix. Promotions may be designed to increase traffic, frequency and amount of purchases, to even out demand, to encourage trial of new products or services, or to counter competition. The range of promotional offers is endless. They include: price-related offers; free extra product or free samples; customer loyalty schemes; contests; and sweepstakes. The commercial organizations in the information marketplace engage in a number of sales promotion activities. Contests and draws are common at trade exhibitions. Special discounts may be available for subscribing to a database over a limited period, or for specific groups of users. For libraries, where revenue is unlikely to be significantly increased through sales promotion, it can be difficult to justify the expenditure, but there are ways in which the user experience might be enhanced for short periods in order to encourage a higher level of participation in information activities. If a workplace library offers lunchtime

125

seminars, with sandwiches, to brief people on new developments in patents and intellectual property, is this sales promotion?

*REFLECT: List some examples of sales promotion activities that might be relevant for a new ICT skills initiative being launched by a public library.*

## EXHIBITIONS

Exhibitions are time-consuming and can be expensive. Nevertheless they are a useful way of making contact with a targeted community. Many organizations that offer services to other libraries or information professionals take the opportunity to exhibit at those exhibitions that attract information professionals. Exhibitions are opportunities to:

- build customer relationships – by meeting customers with whom communication is normally by phone or e-mail. Contacts may also be made with potential customers;
- display new products – by demonstrating and discussing new products and services with existing and potential customers. At exhibitions visitors have a sense of purpose and absorption that would be difficult to achieve in the workplace; they are there to gather information and to make contacts.
- learn about the marketplace – by meeting representatives of other exhibitors or partners in collaborative ventures, and examining stands, in terms of both products and promotional messages;
- build market presence – by participating, the organization is demonstrating a commitment to the market, to presence, and to interaction with the exhibition audience;
- create PR spin-offs – which arise from using the exhibition in other forms of promotion, such as press releases, advertising ('See us at stand 200'), direct mail (including exhibition details and tickets).

Public library business information services might typically participate in a business exhibition; library consortia and national libraries may exhibit at library technology or Internet exhibitions; but for other libraries exhibition stands at smaller events may be more appropriate. An academic library might set up a stand in public concourse areas to encourage the use of new Web-based subject gateway services. The library of a professional body might use a small portable stand that can be erected at any meeting of members or potential customers. All organizations have a use for a portable exhibition stand, publicity packs, and a portable PC (to demonstrate access to services or support a simple presentation). Roadshows are a further option for the more ambitious.

## SPONSORSHIP

Sponsorship is the provision of financial or material support by an organization for some independent activity not directly linked with the organization's normal business; the organization expects to benefit from this support. The main purpose of sponsorship is to generate positive attitudes by associating a corporate name with sport, the arts, a charitable enterprise or some other community or high-profile activities. The sponsor hopes to benefit through media coverage of sponsored events and initiatives. Libraries are more likely to be the recipients of sponsorship than the initiators, but in a world where partnerships and collaboration are commonplace, it may sometimes be difficult to differentiate between the sponsor and the recipient! Sponsorship may take the form of monetary support, but sponsorship in kind is also widespread. Recent examples from the public library sector include: free advertising space for a special event; materials for a summer playscheme; and structural steel for building an art gallery and library.

## PERSONAL SELLING

In one sense personal selling is the channel of least relevance to library–user relationships in the information marketplace, but in another sense it underpins the embedding of marketing orientation. It is therefore appropriate to conclude this chapter with a few comments on personal selling.

Personal selling is an interpersonal communication tool which involves face-to-face activities undertaken by individuals, often representing an organization, to inform, persuade or remind an individual or group to take appropriate action, as required by the sponsor's representative. The particular attraction of personal selling is that, unlike any of the other promotion mix elements, it is the basis for a two-way, interactive dialogue between buyer and seller.

Personal selling generally has a much more important role in the sale of a high-priced infrequently purchased industrial good than in the sale of a routinely purchased consumer product, but estate agents and car salesmen are good examples of personal selling in the consumer marketplace. What relevance does personal selling have in library and information contexts, since a sale is not normally in prospect and consumer interactions tend to be more concerned with a series of ongoing transactions than a significant one-off decision or interaction? In the information industry most individuals combine selling with other roles. Examples are sales consultants for publishers and library management systems, who often also have training roles. To generalize the concept of personal selling, if an organization subscribes to a marketing orientation, all staff, and especially front-line service staff, are salespeople, and every transaction should be approached as a sales transaction. Figure 7.11 lists the stages in the personal selling process. These stages are a useful guide to the steps in any interaction with a user. The first, prospecting, is concerned with understanding the user and their needs; preparation and planning use this understanding to develop services and knowledge that will ensure that responses to user requests are effective and efficient. Users may need to be encouraged to interact with staff, particularly in initiating contact. Responding to user requests can be seen as a sales presentation, and needs to be professionally delivered, with an eye to the impact that this interaction will have on the continuation of an effective relationship with the user. Handling objections and negotiation are perhaps more appropriately interpreted as the stages concerned with supporting a dialogue, and, where appropriate, supporting learning. The transaction is completed when the user is satisfied, but in closing the sale foundations must be laid for the continuation of the relationship.

## REAFFIRMING THE MESSAGE

All aspects of service delivery communicate an image to customers. Signage, condition and ambience of the building, furniture, reliability of computer equipment, prompt answering of telephone calls and even the cleanliness of the toilets will affect users' perceptions of the organization. Ultimately, marketing messages must be reinforced by and consistent with the customer's experience.

- Prospecting
- Preparation and planning
- Initiating contact
- Sales presentation
- Handling objectives
- Negotiation
- Closing the sale
- Follow-up and account management

**Figure 7.11**   Stages in the personal selling process

# CONCLUSION

Promotion is an important component of the marketing mix. Promotional approaches include advertising, direct marketing, sales promotions, public relations and publicity, personal selling and sponsorship. The design of appropriate communication strategies involves a number of considerations, for example the target audience, communication objectives and the marketing message. Next, factors associated with the 'how' need attention. This involves the selection of communication channels, budget-setting and the design of the promotional mix. Finally, it is necessary to measure the outcome of promotional endeavours in order to establish whether the investment in promotion has been worthwhile, and to inform the commitment to and nature of future promotional activities.

A number of the elements in the promotional mix have been reviewed in this chapter. Although it has surveyed a wide range of options, approaches that are appropriate where marketing budgets are limited are specifically identified. The elements of the promotional mix that have been considered include: public relations, direct marketing, advertising, sales promotion, exhibitions, sponsorship and personal selling.

# REFERENCES AND FURTHER READING

Coote, H. and Batchelor, B. (1997), *How to Market your Library Service Effectively.* 2nd edition. London: Aslib. (Aslib Know How Guide, ed. Sylvia Webb.)

De Mooij, M. (1994), *Advertising Worldwide: Concepts, Theories and Practice of International, Multinational and Global Advertising.* 2nd edition. Englewood Cliffs, NJ: Prentice Hall.

Dibb, S., Simkin, L., Pride, W.M. and Ferrell, O.C. (1994), *Marketing Concepts and Strategies.* Boston and London: Houghton Mifflin.

Fill, C. (1995), *Marketing Communication: Frameworks, Theories and Applications.* Prentice Hall.

Hanson, W. (2000) *Principles of Internet Marketing.* Cincinnati, OH: South-Western College Publishing.

Hart, K. (1999), *Putting Marketing Ideas into Action.* London: Library Association. (The Successful LIS Professional, ed. Sheila Pantry.)

Hooley, G. and Lynch, J.E. (1985), 'How UK advertisers set budgets', *International Journal of Advertising*, **3**, 223–31.

Mercer, D. (1996), *Marketing.* 2nd edition. Oxford: Blackwell.

Peterson, R.A. (1997), *Electronic Marketing and the Consumer.* Thousand Oaks, CA and London: Sage.

Rossiter, J.R. and Percy, L. (1987), *Advertising and Promotion Management.* New York: McGraw-Hill.

Smith, P.R. (1993), *Marketing Communications*, Kogan Page.

White, R. (1988), *Advertising: What it is and How to do it.* New York: McGraw-Hill.

# 8  Price and pricing policy

## AIMS

Price is a key element in the marketing mix, and has a significant effect on the operation of the information marketplace. This chapter:

- explores the role of price;
- discusses the classical relationship between price and supply and demand;
- emphasizes the role of pricing objectives;
- reviews the factors affecting pricing decisions, and discusses how these affect the pricing of information products; and
- explains the different approaches to pricing policy, including the principles and expectations associated with free access to information at the point of use, and the role of portals on the Web.

## INTRODUCTION

> No one should think that the area of pricing, particularly of newer forms of information products and services, is stable or that there are any simple guidelines. Product pricing is fluid, changing and rather uncertain as technology is changing the relative economics of traditional forms of publication against optical media, and of on-line databases versus CD-ROMs, and so on. The market is in flux and only a limited number of significant players are yet making profits from these services. (Brindley, 1993, p. 297)

Although this statement was made in 1993, and in the meantime the technological basis may have shifted from CD-ROM to Web-based delivery of information products, it is echoed in the comments that are currently being made about e-business. Yet pricing is traditionally recognized to play a central role in the functioning of the economic system. The three macroeconomic functions of price are:

1. Allocation or rationing, or the balancing of the quantities demanded and those supplied.
2. Stimulation and acting as an incentive for new players and products to enter a marketplace.
3. Distribution, whereby income is distributed between buyers and sellers.

The price mechanism is the dominant force in resource allocation, income distribution and size and composition of output. Pricing for information products, then, plays a significant role in availability and access to those products, and is central to the concept of an information society. Yet both commentators on the information marketplace (for example Arnold, 1990) and those writing on pricing decisions in general (for example Lancioni and Gattorna, 1993) agree that whilst the pricing decision has a direct impact on profit, and on all other elements of the marketing mix, price planning is one of the most overlooked and poorly understood areas of marketing. In the public sector, the key issue is often the rationing of resources. Price and charging can be used as a rationing device to control demand for some services.

Whilst pricing of traditional print-based information products and the services based upon them presents some challenges, the pricing of electronic information is a nightmare. The risk associated with pricing electronic information for a consumer marketplace has driven journal publishers, reference book and database publishers into the arms of the library consortia, and looks set to confirm a future for libraries as intermediaries in the information marketplace. Not only is the advent of e-commerce changing pricing levels; it is revolutionizing business models. A good example is *Encyclopedia Britannica*, the print version of which was priced as a prestige product and generated significant revenues for its publishers over many years. *Britannica* is now free to consumers on the Web, and revenue comes from advertisements and other commercial ventures. The acquisition of *Britannica* by a major portal provider in order to enhance the information content of its portal makes commercial sense.

Why is price important in the information marketplace? The answer to this question requires a consideration of price in both profit and non-profit situations. The information industry embraces publishers, online hosts, database producers and other service suppliers that function as commercial organizations. Many of these businesses supply other businesses or libraries in the academic and public library sectors with information products. Price is a component of the contract in these organizational relationships. These businesses also offer services to individual consumers at a price. For these organizations, price is clearly an important factor in continuing commercial viability. Within workplace libraries, pricing may be an issue that arises in the context of re-charge mechanisms between departments, but it is unlikely that the end-user of a service will be charged. Some organizations, most notably public and academic libraries, are not for profit. In this context price can be understood in a number of different ways. Sometimes prices are charged for selected services, such as a business information service or interlibrary loans. These services may be regarded as additional to the basic public service, and it may be viewed appropriate to recoup costs or, alternatively, prices may be set in order to encourage the user to value the service more highly. On other occasions, allocation is by other criteria, such as perceived need, but even in these circumstances it is still necessary to understand the value that the customer places on the service and also, on occasions, to understand the 'price' to the user in accessing the service in terms, for example, of sacrifices of time and energy. Increasingly, Internet portals are offering information content free, in order to create and maintain a customer community.

*REFLECT: List the priced products or services that are offered by your information service.*

In general, consumers appear reluctant to pay for information, preferring either to do without or to collect it from some free source. However, when they perceive it to be of great significance they tend to seek information and advice, or evaluated information, and are prepared to pay considerable sums to financial consultants, accountants, legal advisers and others. They will, however, pay for information products, such as books, journals and newspapers. Pricing of information is not an issue in those arenas in which the consumer is not prepared to pay. Many of the information needs of individuals are met through organizations, such as their employer or a library. The quality of the services that these agencies are able to offer depends crucially on the pricing of information. Pricing in the information marketplace, as distinct from other aspects of marketing, is primarily associated with organizational marketing.

## THE THEORY OF SUPPLY AND DEMAND

From a microeconomic perspective, or the perspective of the individual organization, price is the single most important decision in marketing. This derives from the fundamental relationship between profit and price, which can be expressed simply as:

Profit = price − cost, on a per unit basis

Sales volume is the other factor that affects profit. This is also intimately related to price, since price affects sales volume. A fuller expression of the relationship between these quantities is represented by the following equation:

$$\text{Profits} = \text{price} \times \text{quantities sold} - \text{total costs}$$

Admittedly these two equations express the relationship in very simple terms. They neglect:

- the realities of portfolio pricing across a group of products;
- investment in the development of products;
- the need to recoup that investment; and
- other more sophisticated financial ratios.

All of the above would need to be taken into account in order to reflect the true effect of price on the financial health of an organization. Nevertheless, the equations do emphasize the intimate relationship between price and profit. Ultimately, the higher the price can be raised, assuming stable unit costs and sales volume, the higher the profit. In both public and private sector organizations higher profit not only heralds higher returns, but in a changing marketplace it offers a much-needed opportunity for reinvestment in technological and other developments, which lend the organization the flexibility it needs to survive.

These basic equations also flag the intimate relationship between price and cost. Issues of costing are not explored in any detail in this text, since it is argued that a range of organizational, customer and market factors determines the way in which organizations distribute costs across their portfolio of products. There are, for example, a number of different algorithms for allocating fixed costs to specific projects or activities. Nevertheless, in all supply chains the cost of one product affects the cost of the next product in the chain, and thereby often influences the range of price options available to the business. Indeed, for electronic information products, the contract normally specifies a use agreement as well as a price, so that any organization that wishes to repackage the information and embed it in another service will be constrained by pricing strategies further up the chain. Snyder and Davenport (1997) offer a useful review of costing issues.

The final relationship that is evident in the above equations is that between profit and the number of units sold. Chapter 9 considers marketing research, which should yield an understanding of the customer needs on which projections of demand can be based. However, especially with new products and changing marketplaces, these estimates may be inaccurate. For example, for new e-information products it is difficult to predict:

- the magnitude and speed of uptake of new products, such as electronic journals;

- the magnitude and speed of the impact that these e-products will have on revenues from print products (remembering that this impact may not always be negative, if complementary products can be delivered through parallel media).

Price is also important in relationships with customers. It is the **value** placed on what is exchanged, representing the value at which a seller is prepared to exchange and the value at which the customer is prepared to participate in that exchange. Something of value, usually buying power, is exchanged for satisfaction or utility. Often that something of value is money, but other commodities of value to both parties may also be exchanged, such as other goods, time or commitment.

Classical economic theory has used the concepts of supply and demand to determine what is described as the **equilibrium price**. Specifically:

- **demand** is the quantity of a good that buyers wish to purchase at each conceivable price;
- **supply** is the quantity of a good that sellers wish to sell at each conceivable price.

If a graph is drawn to show supply and demand curves, the point of intersection of those curves determines the equilibrium price, or the price at which the exchange will take place. **Price** is seen as the balance between supply and demand.

This model works well in pure commodity markets with undifferentiated products (that is, products that are all the same, such as water or coal), but in real markets a number of the assumptions that underlie this model present problems:

1. The model assumes that the buyer has near perfect information about the alternatives and the market; a buyer is rarely that well informed (although some believe that things may be different in e-marketplaces).
2. The model assumes that competing brands are reasonably close substitutes for one another. In real markets, suppliers devote considerable effort through strategies such as branding to differentiate their products, or to encourage consumers to view their product as different, in some way, from those of their competitors.
3. The model assumes that the demand curve is known; this is rarely the case because suppliers are rarely in a position to be able to test the market at different price levels.
4. The model takes no account of the ongoing costs of a purchase, such as subsequent subscriptions or maintenance costs, and focuses only on the initial cost.

It is hypothesized that real demand shows a steep demand curve and a two-part supply curve. In other words, demand is very dependent on (or elastic in respect of) price, and below a certain price suppliers are reluctant to enter the marketplace. Once that price has been achieved, many competitors may enter the marketplace, and thus supply may outstrip demand; in time, this will have a corresponding effect on price.

The relationship between supply and demand and price may also be influenced by the extent to which competition is based on price. In price competition, price is emphasized to the consumer as an issue and organizations will seek to attract customers away from their competitors on the basis of price. In such an environment, an organization needs to be confident that it is a low-cost producer. Price is an easy variable to change, but if competitors respond similarly, then a price war results, and profitability for the industry drops. Accordingly, key players in a marketplace may explicitly or implicitly collude to avoid a price war.

Non-price competition, on the other hand, is based on distinctive product features, services, quality, promotion, and/or packaging. In such markets, although differentiation may not be based on price, price is still critical, and may act as a qualifying factor.

Information products have medium fixed costs and almost zero variable costs. Variable cost therefore plays a minimal role in determining profit, but amplifies the importance of knowing and understanding what customers are willing to pay. Marketing managers should focus on achieving accurate estimates of demand. Another factor that affects demand for information products is that people generally only buy one copy, and do not make repeat purchases of the same item.

*REFLECT: What factors other than price would be considered in the following decision-making situations:*

1. *A library acquiring a children's book on the Romans*
2. *A parent seeking items to support a child undertaking a project on the Romans.*

## PRICING OBJECTIVES

The first step that an organization needs to take in establishing its pricing strategies is to determine the objectives that it wishes thereby to achieve. These are called pricing objectives. Any such objectives must be consistent with the organization's overall objectives as expressed, for example, in its strategic plan. In addition, pricing objectives support marketing objectives. Many organizations seek to achieve more than one pricing objective simultaneously.

Some typical pricing objectives are:

- Survival in the medium to long term, which depends on visibility and products that are valued by customers
- Increased or maintained level of profitability
- Achievement of a specified level of return on investment (ROI), or a specific value of some other measure of financial performance
- Retention or increase of market share, which ensures an established customer base for the future, whether the agenda is public service or commercial gain
- Cash flow and liquidity, so that the organization is in a position to stay in business. Break-even often constrains public sector organizations and projects
- Creation of illusions of high product quality, and the related issue of strengthening the brand and relationships with customers.

Such objectives are often set and reviewed on an annual basis, but underlying strategic objectives that drive pricing objectives are likely to be stable over several years. Timescales for pricing objectives associated with specific projects will be influenced by project timescales.

## FACTORS AFFECTING PRICING DECISIONS

A number of factors might affect pricing decisions and determine the approach to pricing policy that is taken. Organizations should take some of these into account when setting their pricing policies, and this introduces a considerable element of judgement and risk into any pricing decisions. Factors can be broadly grouped into organizational factors, customer factors and market factors. Organizations should consider the resources available to them, and how they can be utilized to support specific pricing policies.

### ORGANIZATIONAL FACTORS

The organizational factors that might influence price decision-making are related to the organization's objectives and resources, coupled with the existing product portfolio and the organization's potential to develop it. Organizational factors that might influence price are described below.

#### Product lifecycle

This refers specifically to the stage that any given product is in its lifecycle. Organizations often choose a **price-skimming** strategy for new products, where the price is set high initially with a view to creating an image of a desirable or quality product. Thus **price-skimming** is charging the highest possible price that buyers who most desire the product will pay. The advantage of price skimming is that development costs can be covered relatively quickly, and demand can be kept consistent with production capacity, or the capacity to support new users of an information service. Booksellers and movie producers frequently exhibit skimming strategies in which initial runs are more expensive (for example hard-cover editions or first-run movies). Over time the price is reduced until the market is saturated.

Later in the product lifecycle, volume sales may require that price be reduced as the product reaches maturity. In addition, a mature market is generally subject to greater price competition. **Penetration price** is a price set below that of competing brands in order to penetrate the market and produce a larger unit sales volume, thus gaining a large market share quickly. This pricing strategy is used for software. More sales means that the software takes on the status of a *de facto* standard, and is therefore more valuable to both the buyer and the supplier. The disadvantage is that the organization subsequently has less flexibility in pricing, because whilst it is easy to lower prices, the market is normally very intolerant of raised prices (unless the initial price is seen as a promotional price). Organizations sometimes use penetration pricing after skimming pricing so that they achieve a large market share if competitors are expected to enter the market quickly. This approach has been used with the introduction of many IT products, such as PCs, printers and scanners.

Decline occurs when the product is no longer attractive to the marketplace at a price which satisfies the suppliers. Many consumer CD-ROM products entered the marketplace at a high price; prices have declined as the size of the market has grown and more entrants have led to more severe competition.

### Portfolio

The nature of the portfolio of products may influence price. Organizations often develop pricing strategies that extend across part or all of their portfolio of products and balance prices across products to optimize achievement of objectives. Large market players are in a particularly strong position to use portfolio pricing. Thus, a dictionary publisher, such as Oxford University Press, may support the initial launch of a CD-ROM product by revenues generated through print products; this in turn must affect the pricing of the print products.

### Product line

Product line pricing is similar to portfolio pricing, but here the price of one product may affect others supplied by the organization, either through interrelated demand, for example hardware and software, or interrelated costs, for example oil and petrol from the same process. Thus the various printed and electronic products generated from a database, such as the INSPEC database, share costs, and prices of some products may be determined by the opportunity to recoup costs on other products.

## Segmentation and product positioning

A prime benefit of segmentation and positioning is the reduction in price pressures deriving from severe competition. Many information products and information services have sought differentiation on the basis of locality or organizational base of users, or quality or subject base of product. Public and academic libraries have uniquely defined core communities. Also there is, for example, very little duplication of major bibliographic databases covering specific subjects in the English language. Nevertheless, parallel products may exist with similar subject coverage but in French or German, designed for linguistically distinct markets. These parallel products are a potential source of future competition. The complexity of pricing strategies in the information industry is a result of some 'benefit' segmentation of organizational, library and consumer markets.

## Cost

Pricing may be based on production costs in a number of ways. Two common approaches are:

- cost-plus pricing
- mark-up pricing.

In **cost-plus pricing** the price is determined by adding a percentage or a fixed amount to the supplier's costs. Cost-plus is suitable when production costs are unpredictable, and in markets in which price competition is not severe (for example government defence contracts). In most marketplaces customers will not tolerate the variability that might be inherent in cost-plus pricing.

In **mark-up pricing** the price is derived by adding a predetermined percentage of the cost. Often different product ranges merit or attract different mark-ups. Mark-up pricing is common in retailing, and is used in book-selling.

Information intermediaries may use either or both of these strategies in, for example, re-charging users for access to online search services or downloading electronic information, but these approaches assume that marginal costing is used as the basis for pricing. In reality it is challenging to calculate the cost of providing a unit of information service, such as a training session, an issue transaction, or a document delivery relating to three journal articles. This is fundamentally because the specific service transaction in which the customer

139

participates is only possible because the library has the resources and expertise to manage access to a large collection of information resources, amongst which is the item, or opportunity to access the item that the user wants.

## CUSTOMER FACTORS

Customer factors also influence price, simply because, as already discussed, there is a close relationship between demand and price. It is not surprising, then, that the main determinant of price from this perspective is the amount the customer is prepared to pay. In information marketplaces there is some reluctance on the part of consumers to pay for some types of information. In these contexts the key issue is the organization's willingness and ability to pay. Customer impact is related to the following factors.

### Inherent or generated demand for a product

Particularly where supply is limited, such as in the housing market or the holiday market, increase in demand will push up the price. This has limited relevance for electronic products, since the essential nature of electronic information is the 'publication-on-demand' facility. Demand may have an effect on price or the value attached to an information product when items are scarce, sure as with rare and ancient books, special collections, and other unique items that are irreplaceable treasures associated with our cultural heritage.

### Demand-oriented pricing

Here the price depends on the anticipated level of demand. Demand-oriented pricing is used in many service sectors, such as the travel industry and the telecommunications industry in order to attempt to level out demand. Effective use of this strategy requires accurate prediction of demand at different price levels and at different times. Demand-oriented pricing allows suppliers to maximize their revenues during times of peak demand, and to make special offers to increase service use during otherwise slack periods. Optimizing revenues across all periods of service delivery means that there is greater potential for profitability than with cost-oriented pricing. Database vendors may try to maximize profit by charging the highest possible price during peak periods whilst offering rebates during periods when demand is lower.

## Benefits

Acceptable price will be determined to a considerable extent by the match between the benefits that the product offers and the benefits that the customer seeks. In particular, a premium price may be set if there are perceived to be additional benefits. Brand loyalty allows the setting of a premium price (see Chapter 6). Thus software suppliers for, say, library management systems, who are known to provide an effective support service and to offer effective upgrades and maintenance of software, are likely to be in a stronger position to charge a premium price than those who do not.

Other added-value features, such as options for downloading information or sharing information with others, may also be perceived as benefits. Speed of delivery is sufficiently important to justify price differentials. Figure 8.1 shows the price differential for a number of document delivery services operating in Australia.

## Value

Benefits can be conceptualized as the value that the customer sees in the product and, in theory, there should be a balance between this and the price asked. The concept of value in relation to information has been debated by Eaton and Bawden (1991). The value of information is not readily quantifiable. It has no intrinsic value. Its value depends upon its context and its use by particular users on particular occasions, and is impossible to determine in advance. It is also difficult to predict how the value will change over time. Accordingly, the concept of value is difficult to define in this context. Nevertheless, it remains true that value can:

| Service | Speed | Cost per item, photocopy (mail/Ariel) | Cost per item, fax/ desktop delivery |
|---|---|---|---|
| DocSS – Standard | 4–6 days | AUS$12 | AUS$15 |
| DocSS – Fast Track | 24 hours | AUS$24 (Ariel or collected) | AUS$27 |
| DocSS – Fast Track Plus | 2 hours | – | AUS$39 |
| ILL | – | Determined by | supplying library |
| Supply 1 | 2–14 days (no guarantee) | AUS$27 | AUS$30 |
| UnCover | 24 hours | – | AUS$14.50 plus variable copyright fee |
| UnCover Express | 60 minutes | – | AUS$14.50 plus variable copyright fee |

**Figure 8.1**  Comparison of National Library of Australia document delivery services

141

- vary between segments, depending to some extent on how the information is used to generate wealth, and this accounts for the differential pricing of information to business and educational establishments. Different values may also be associated with different types of databases, and this leads to differential pricing between, for example, bibliographic databases, full-text databases, humanities databases and company databanks. If differential prices are set for different segments it must be possible to categorize customers into clearly defined segments, and, for electronic information, to ensure that customers in segments benefiting from lower prices cannot resell information to or share information with those in higher-priced segments;
- buyers may have a range of acceptable prices, known as the 'reference price range', for a product type. They are unlikely to make a purchase outside this range. In some cases these prices are determined by what the customer is used to paying, such as 10p for a photocopy or a telephone call.

### Distribution

In many instances, producers do not interact directly with consumers. Database producers may make information available through online hosts or CD-ROM publishers who act as 'retailers' and give the individual product more visibility as part of a portfolio of comparable products. In such circumstances, producers cannot determine the final price to the end-user or consumer because the intermediaries apply their own pricing strategies. Intermediaries will want to control their margins and to determine other elements of their relationship with the supplier, such as discounts for large orders, sale or return, support with promotion and so on. Exclusive distribution in the wider consumer market often means that both the producer and the distributor can benefit from higher prices.

### MARKET FACTORS

Two components of the market, competition and the marketing environment, are also important factors in pricing decisions.

### Competition

Price decision-making must take into account the prices set by competitors. This includes not only direct competitors or those producing similar products, but also indirect competition from different products that might meet the same needs or offer the same benefits. So, for example, some public library services are concerned with leisure and, in this context, public libraries should consider the wider costs and benefits to the public of the library as a leisure activity, compared with the services offered by other providers of leisure activities. An organization may choose between charging the same price, undercutting the price charged by the opposition, or presenting the service as better in some way so that higher prices can realistically be set.

**Competition-oriented pricing** may be used to achieve a range of objectives, for example to increase market share or to enter a new market segment.

*REFLECT: Compare a visit to a public library with a visit to the local swimming baths as a leisure experience.*

### Environment

A range of social, technological, economic and political factors may shape the marketplace in which a producer operates. These may influence price. So, for example, inflation will often cause prices to rise, whilst recession in which both public and consumer spending is under tight constraints is likely to lead to price cuts. The interesting feature of the wider information market is that it is an international marketplace, so that international trade and economic trends may have an overall impact, yet individual players will be differentially affected by the changes in national markets consistent with their market share in those individual markets. Such fluctuations may affect their behaviour in either or both of local and global marketplaces. Journal publishers suffered a few years ago when there were significant currency fluctuations between countries, which made journals from publishers based in countries with strong currencies difficult to afford in countries with weaker currencies. This has a corresponding effect on publishers' sales and revenues.

**Historical pricing** takes one significant element of the environment into account when raising or changing prices. Customers, especially organizational customers, who have records of how much they paid the previous year, may consider whether they wish to continue a relationship with an information provider if the gap between a previous price and a proposed price is too great. A sharp increase in pricing is an invitation to consider switching.

## SOME PRICING STRATEGIES IN THE INFORMATION MARKETPLACE

As indicated above, a wide range of factors should be taken into account when determining price and approaches to pricing. Typically, the organization will use some of these in complex pricing models designed to achieve the pricing objectives of the organization. For some products, such as books or the consumer market for CD-ROMs, there will be a list price for the item, which is set after consideration of the pricing objectives, including financial and marketplace performance objectives. Pricing strategies for electronic information products are notably more complex, and a number of different approaches to pricing and payment for access to databases and to electronic document delivery have been tried. The early online search services based pricing on combinations of connect-time charges, display/print charges, telecommunication charges and charges for special services. This model has to some extent been superseded by approaches based upon subscriptions, contracts with consortia, and pay-as-you-go. Another very significant difference between print-based information products and electronic information products, where payment is on the basis of access (rather than subscription), is that the customer pays for the print product in advance; online information on a pay-as-you-go basis is paid for when it is retrieved, or after. This raises the issue of the point at which the customer pays for the information product, the effect that this has on the consumer's purchase decision-making behaviour, and specifically their attitude to price. Key approaches to pricing in the information industry are discussed further below.

## ITEM-BASED PRICING

Information products that are sold as one-off items to the consumer market, such as books, a local history publication or a tourist guide of an area, will have a set price. This list price is typically a recommended price set by the publisher. The same book will normally be sold at a different price to the library market-place. Different editions may be available at different prices in different countries, and different versions (for example a large-print version or a talking-book version). In addition, different retailers may set their prices differently, as is very evident in the e-marketplace for books. So, although the price level may vary, and different prices are set for different versions and different market segments, the consumer pays an agreed price for the item.

## PAY-FOR-USE

A variation on item-based pricing that is used for electronic information is where the user pays for the information when it is accessed. A business information Website, for example, may provide access to some information free, but should an individual wish to download a list of several thousand addresses for marketing purposes, the user will be charged for this on the basis of the information that has been downloaded. Similarly, document delivery services allow consumers to order journal articles through their Web-based services. The end-user will be charged for the item ordered. Payment may be by credit card, e-cash, or account

**Dialog Alert Service**

Dialog Alert profiles bring you regular updates of the most recent information available. They run each time a database is updated and deliver results via a delivery method of your choice (fax, mail, e-mail) automatically, without any ongoing effort on your part.

Charges for Dialog Alert profiles vary, depending on the source database, frequency of Alert run (e.g., daily, weekly), and delivery method. Up to 20 prints per profile per update are included, except as noted in the Database Rates section of the Price List. No charge is incurred for search terms or DialUnits. For prints over 20 or for profiles without prints included, prints are charged at current Price List rates for the specified database and format. To check Dialog Alert pricing for a database, enter HELP RATES nnn, where nnn is the file number.

**Dialog Interactive Alerts**

Dialog provides an interactive alerting service with subscriptions to predefined strategies covering top publications and newsletters. The pricing for this service has two components: the **Flat Delivery Fee** for distributing Interactive Titles Lists and articles to recipients' e-mail boxes and the **Article Fees** for the specific articles ordered. Dialog Interactive Alerts charges are part of your total Dialog usage and are billed on the monthly Dialog invoice. See our Web site for more information.

**Flat Delivery Fee**

The monthly Flat Delivery Fee is based on an account's total number of active subscriptions. There are no additional charges for the delivery of Interactive Titles Lists and articles, regardless of the number of recipients or the number of articles ordered.

| # of Subscriptions | Monthly flat delivery fee |
|---|---|
| 1–10 | $10.00 |
| 11–30 | $20.00 |
| Over 30 | $30.00 |

**Article Fees**

Full-text article fees vary by database and are based on the current published Dialog database rates. For multiple copies, our redistribution feature will calculate the charges depending on the number of copies requested by your company.

**Figure 8.2** Pricing strategies for Dialog Alert Service (a current-awareness service)

and invoice. Figure 8.2, which shows pricing strategies for Dialog Alert Service, a current-awareness service, demonstrates that the pricing for the current-awareness service is a flat monthly fee, whereas charges for the full-text articles are on a pay-per-item basis, and depend on the database from which they are extracted.

Tips on how to price a library publication are given in Figure 8.3.

## SUBSCRIPTIONS

Subscriptions are a well-established means of ensuring a more persistent commitment to a periodical publication, such as a journal, a magazine or a newspaper. In consumer markets, subscriptions encourage customer loyalty and ensure

1. Determine pricing objectives, e.g. to cover costs or to make a profit, and reflect on the level of risk that is acceptable in respect of any losses.
2. Calculate the cost of production, including any physical production costs, and if deemed appropriate, staff time devoted to the project.
3. Estimate sales, based on the sale of previous publications, or the size of the potential audience. Size may depend on the potential outlets, such as whether sale will be through a special event, or through a museum and library bookstand. Calculate print run on the basis of this estimate of sales.
4. Estimate sales revenue, at different levels of sales, such as 50 percent, 75 per cent and 100 per cent.
5. Taking into account the acceptable level of risk, choose an estimated figure for sales revenue.
6. Calculate units costs and unit sales revenue and, taking into account the pricing objectives, set a price.

**Figure 8.3**   Practical tips on how to price a library publication

some stability of revenue over a period of, say, a year. In the library marketplace, libraries have always sought to build a set of all of the issues of periodical publications that are of interest to their clientele, and journal subscription agents have managed the interface between libraries and publishers. Many online services are available on a subscription basis. Such subscription arrangements are often designed to encompass options for both individual consumer subscriptions and subscriptions by libraries, where the library typically provides access to a number of users, possibly located at a range of different sites. Business information providers that have an identifiable business customer base within specific industry sectors, such as LEXIS/NEXIS, have favoured the subscription model for the provision of access to business, company and financial information resources.

## CONTRACTS

Access to electronic information, such as large bibliographic databases, electronic journal collections and business, statistical and other databanks, is increasingly provided to the end-user through libraries. Libraries in both the academic and public sector have formed consortia, which are increasingly functioning as powerful purchasing consortia in negotiation with information providers. Contracts, which embrace price and licensing arrangements, and specify how the information that has been acquired may be used, are agreed and reviewed, typically on an annual basis. Individual libraries then have contracts with the consortia for access to all the negotiated products, or an agreed subset. The advantages of such contracts to the information provider are a guaranteed revenue stream and visibility in the marketplace through association with significant academic and public libraries. In addition, licensing arrangements include controls on the use of the information, which ensures protection of intellectual property. Whilst such controls would be almost impossible to police with individual end-consumers, it is in the interest of all parties in the consortia arrangement to take steps to honour the contractual terms that relate to the acceptable use of the licensed information. For libraries and their users the advantages of the consortium arrangement are wider access to electronic information and support in its acquisition and use from the consortium and other members of the consortium.

Such consortia may also use their purchasing power with publishers when negotiating on the price of print material, computer equipment and various other items necessary to maintain effective information service points.

## CD-ROM PRICING

CD-ROM pricing in consumer marketplaces is straightforward, although there may be some challenges in setting the level of the price if the CD-ROM is likely to undermine sales of a parallel print product, such as an encyclopedia. However, when CD-ROMs are acquired by a library, the issue of multiple use arises. Most libraries acquire information on CD-ROM with a view to making the information available across a network. Publishers have sought to charge libraries for different levels of use and typically have pricing tariffs which specify:

- the number of users to which the network applies; each CD-ROM provider typically has different bands for numbers of users;
- the extent of the network to which a licence can be applied, such as within a building or across a local area network;
- whether or not users are specified as simultaneous users, and therefore whether the number of workstations is a consideration.

In addition, CD-ROM prices may be subject to discounts of various different kinds. These typically relate to:

- parallel print subscriptions
- a renewal price for existing customers that is lower than the initial subscription price
- discounts for subscriptions placed within a limited time
- discounts for non-profit organizations, or for members if a database is compiled by a professional body
- multi-year discounts when pre-paying for multiple years
- discounts for bundled packages of databases and services, possibly including some free online access to databases.

## FREE INFORMATION

'The belief that no one should be excluded from access to information is fundamental to our democratic society' (Olaison, 1992, p. 239). Public libraries and other public sector information providers are engaged on a mission which is concerned with the provision of information in support of the public good, specifically interpreted in terms of the political drivers associated with the creation of the emerging knowledge-based society. Information is a key resource in lifelong learning and ICT for all.

Public libraries have always needed to make a distinction between those activities that are fundamental for all citizens and those services (such as those to business) that could be regarded as added-value services for the benefit of specific segments of their community, and for which it might be appropriate to charge. Both public and academic libraries often charge for photocopying, some types of online or Web searching, interlibrary loans and document delivery from remote collections, but offer a free core service. Academic libraries may offer basic access free to alumni, but charge for other more personalized services. Figure 8.4 summarizes the difference between public and private goods.

As discussed at the beginning of this chapter, many businesses have commercial reasons for providing information free. Increasingly information is provided to consumers as part of the augmented product, or to lubricate the wheels of the relationship between the consumer and the retailer or producer. The use of information in building communities and attracting attention is most evident in the Web portals that are being established by increasing numbers of organizations. Such portals are interested in increasing traffic to their site, and use information among other features to entice consumers to make repeat visits. See Figure 8.5 for BT's Timesmart example.

|  | Private good | Public good |
|---|---|---|
| Exclusion of someone who does not pay | Easy | Difficult |
| Impact of use on supply | Depletes supply | Supply depends on resources |
| Individuals' choice of consumption | Choice | Limited choice |
| Individuals' choice of kind and quality of services | Choice | Limited choice |
| Payment relationship to demand and consumption | Close relationship | Distant relationship |
| Mode of allocation decisions | By market mechanism | By political process |

**Figure 8.4** The difference between private and public goods

Audience: the chronically overworked and congenitally busy
Contents:
1. Toolbox – UK telephone directory, links to Yellow Pages and Spree, a shopping gizmo, reference information, weather maps, currency converters and a world clock
2. Newsfeeds, from Reuters, with stories relayed on the basis of a personal profile
3. Information on timesaving, from *The Sunday Times* and *The Times*, and a programme from Talk Sport radio.
4. BuySmart, a shopping and services area aimed at homeworkers
5. Coffee Break section, including *Times* crossword, daily sports news and a games area, with BT's Gameplay service
6. BT Service centre, showing Friends and Family numbers, phone bill and other services.

**Figure 8.5**   Information for free – BT's Timesmart Web portal

## PROFESSIONAL PRICING

Professional pricing is determined by custom and practice within the industry. So, for example, prescription charges are set at a standard rate, conventions for estate agents are that the fee is a percentage of the selling price of the house, and fees for dentists are determined by a scale. Information consultants may estimate their fees on the basis of an hourly rate that they judge to be the going rate. Professional pricing is important because it reflects the way in which customers expect to be charged for professional services. By operating in accordance with what the customer expects the professionalism of the organizations is confirmed.

## PROMOTIONAL PRICING

Special pricing tactics may be adopted in association with a promotion that is designed to draw attention to a product. From the customer relationship point of view, promotional pricing is designed to encourage switching from a competitor's products. In the information industry this is most evident with promotions on special configurations of hardware. The options are:

- **Price leaders**, which are priced below the usual mark-up at a level near or below cost; revenue from other items should offset these cuts. Major current-awareness services based on the contents pages of journals are offered free in order to encourage purchase or acquisition of journal articles or books from the document suppliers.
- **Special-event pricing**, which is intended to increase sales volume and generate operating capital. A sale or price-cutting linked to a special event are examples of special-event prices. Exhibition offers to subscribe to an information product within one month of visiting the exhibition are an example.

149

## CONCLUSION

This chapter has considered a number of aspects of pricing, including the classical relationship between price and supply and demand, pricing objectives, and factors affecting pricing decisions. Approaches to pricing information products include: item-based pricing; pay-for-use; subscriptions; contracts; CD-ROM pricing; free information; professional pricing; and promotional pricing.

Pricing of information products is complex and fluid in both consumer and business marketplaces. This generates significant challenges for both information providers (at whatever point they are in the supply chain) and users as follows:

1. Publishers, producers and other vendors in the information industry would be in a stronger business position if they were better able to estimate potential revenues.
2. Purchasers, be they end-users or library and information services, like to be able both to compare the price of one information product with another and to predict likely future investment required in an information product of a continuing nature, such as a journal, before initial commitment.

## REFERENCES AND FURTHER READING

Arnold, S.E. (1990), 'Marketing electronic information: theory, practice and challenges 1980–1990', in *Annual Review of Information Science and Technology*, **25**, ed. M.E. Williams. Amsterdam and Oxford: Elsenerfar ASIS, pp. 87–144.

Barker, F. (1984), 'Pricing of information products', *Aslib Proceedings*, **36** (7/8), July–August, 289–97.

Boulding, K. (1968), 'Knowledge as a commodity', in *Beyond Economics: Essays on Society, Religion and Ethics*. Ann Arbor, MI: University of Michigan Press.

Brindley, L.J. (1993), 'Information service and information product pricing', *Aslib Proceedings*, **45** (11/12), November–December, 297–305.

Brown, D, (1993), 'Acquiring electronic documents', in *Taming the Electronic Jungle; Electronic Information: the Collection Management Issues*, ed. M. Morley and H. Woodward. Leeds: National Acquisitions Group and United Kingdom Serials Group.

Butcher, D.R. and Rowley, J.E. (1994), 'A comparison of pricing strategies for bibliographical databases on CD-ROM and equivalent printed products', *The Electronic Library*, **12** (3), June, 169–75.

Butcher, D. and Rowley, J.E. (1996), 'Pricing strategies for business information on CD-ROMs', *Journal of Information Science*, **22** (1), 39–46.

Dunn, J.A. and Martin, M.S. (1994), 'The whole cost of libraries', *Library Trends*, **42** (3), 564–78.

Eaton, J.J. and Bawden, D. (1991), 'What kind of resource is information?', *International Journal of Information Management*, **11**, 156–65.

Fisher, M.T. (1988), 'Overview of pricing strategies in the electronic information industry', *Information Services and Use*, **8** (2/3/4), 73–8.

Hauge, A.O. (1986), 'A strategic appraisal of electronic information marketing, based on experience from Scandinavia', in *Online Information 86*. Proceedings of the 10th International Online Meeting. Oxford: Learned Information (Europe) Ltd, pp. 284–92.

King, C. and Oppenheim, C. (1994), 'Marketing of online and CD-ROM databases', *Online + CDROM Review*, **18** (1), 15–22.

Kingsma, B. (1996), *The Economics of Information*. Englewood: Libraries Unlimited.

Koeing, M.E.D. (1993), 'Two CD-ROM pricing issues', *Online + CDROM Review*, **17** (6), 369–71.

Lancioni, D. and Gattorna, J. (1993), 'Pricing for profit', *Management Research News*, **16** (7), 1–4.

Olaison, J.L. (1992), 'Pricing strategies for library and information services', in Blaise Cronin, ed., *The Marketing of Library and Information Services*. London: Aslib, pp. 238–78.

Rowley, J.E. (1993a), 'Pricing strategy for electronic information: some lessons from online and CD-ROM', *Perspectives in Information Management*, **3** (2), 89–94.

Rowley, J.E. (1993b), 'How much will my online search cost? A review of the changing policies of the online hosts', *Online + CDROM Review*, **17** (3), 143–8.

Rowley, J.E. (1994), 'The price of electronic document delivery', in *Online Information 94*; Proceedings of the 18th International Online Information Meeting. Oxford: Learned Information, pp. 275–84.

Rowley, J.E. (1995), 'Issues in pricing strategies for electronic information', *Pricing and Pricing Strategy: An International Journal*, **3** (2), 4–13.

Rowley, J.E. (1997), 'Pricing and the marketing environment for electronic information', *Journal of Library and Information Science*, **29** (2), 95–102.

Snyder, H. and Davenport, E. (1997), *Costing and Pricing in the Digital Age: a Practical Guide for Information Services*. London: Library Association Publishing.

Unruh, B. and Schipper, W. (1991), 'Pricing marketing, customer support and legal implications', in *Information Distribution Issues for the 90s*. Philadelphia: NFAIS.

Webber, S. (1993), 'Charging for information: some hints', *Inform*, July/August, 3–4.

# 9 Collecting marketing data

## AIMS

Marketing research and information systems are key approaches in the collection of marketing data. They provide insights into customer requirements and an awareness of the changing marketing environment, and help to inform better decision-making about all aspects of marketing strategies. This chapter:

- explores the role of marketing research and marketing information systems;
- identifies marketing research questions and approaches to marketing research studies;
- discusses the collection of primary and secondary marketing research data;
- reviews the issues associated with the collection of secondary data;
- explores data collection methods for primary research; and
- explains the role and types of marketing information systems.

## INTRODUCTION

Organizations need to collect data and information concerning customers, markets and the marketing environment. Marketing research is the term used to refer to the systematic collection of such data. It shares many characteristics of other research endeavours, and some of the same approaches and methodologies may be adopted. Its unique feature is that the enquiry is focused on the collection of information that may support an organization in the marketing of one or several of its products. Libraries have a long tradition of user surveys, that investigate information and information-searching behaviour and collect information about behaviour and attitudes. They are a major category of marketing research activity in the information service contexts, and share principles and approaches with other marketing research endeavours. Marketing research can be viewed as one part of the two-way communication process with customers.

Promotion is concerned with communication from the organization to the customer, and market research facilitates communication from the customer or potential customer to the organization. This customer-based information flow may also be supplemented by information from other sources relating to the marketplace. Marketing research is concerned with the collection of information, but it also forms part of the dialogue between the organization and its customers. It helps organizations and their managers to understand the marketing environment, and to make better-informed decisions about marketing strategies. Formal market research is particularly valuable for producers, such as publishers, which often sell their products through intermediaries or retailers and are thus one step removed from direct dialogue with their customers. In addition, formal market research can help to divide large consumer markets into manageable segments, and then gather information on the needs and interests of those segments, and how their members can be reached with promotional activities. One of the tools used in the marketing research process is the marketing information system. Recent technological opportunities have led to developments such as database marketing, loyalty cards and Internet retailing. All these approaches can be viewed as components of relationship marketing, and may be used to enhance the organization's ability to anticipate and respond to individual customer needs. Indeed, market research may merge with service evaluation (as discussed in Chapter 4) and other approaches which seek to monitor customer responses to offerings. Many of the approaches and techniques described in this chapter are also applicable where customer reactions and behaviour need to be investigated. In the next section we therefore offer some definitions of both market research and marketing information systems and databanks. The chapter then considers types of marketing research questions and a range of approaches to the collection of primary and secondary marketing research data. Finally, the role of marketing information systems is discussed.

Marketing research may seem too grand a concept for a small knowledge centre in a medium-sized business, and alien to an academic library that works in close collaboration with academic staff. In such situations appreciation of customer needs is gathered in the process of service delivery through conversations with users and in discussions in meetings; it may be largely informal. These channels yield important qualitative insights (not unlike those that may emerge in formally constituted focus groups), which are difficult to draw out through some of the more formal marketing research techniques, and would be unlikely to become evident through the analysis of the data in a marketing information system. Even in such circumstances, and others in which the customer group is closely defined (as is often the case in organizational marketing), some of the techniques explored in this chapter are useful. They may, for example, be employed in the formal evaluation of new products and services, or in profiling, with more accuracy than informal methods permit, the significance of an issue across a group of users.

At the other end of the scale, large marketing research projects undertaken before launching a new product may involve regulatory and standards bodies, partners, and marketing research agencies, as well as the organization commissioning the research. Marketing research agencies serve the retail industry with both one-off investigations and regular reporting of customer responses, and these agencies form a significant element in the information industry.

*REFLECT: How does your organization collect information about its customers and their preferences?*

## DEFINITIONS

**Marketing research** is concerned with collecting information so that an organization can better understand its marketplace and its customers. Collecting information on the actual and potential marketplace not only allows the organization to monitor trends and issues relating to its current customers, but also enables it to profile potential new customers and new markets. The better the planning, data collection, information management and analysis, the more reliable and useful will be the outputs, and the better equipped the organization will be to respond to the changing environment in which it operates. Marketing research can be defined as:

> the systematic design, collection, interpretation and reporting of information to help marketers solve specific marketing problems or to take advantage of marketing opportunities.

Important features of this definition are that market research is concerned with the collection of information on a special project basis, and with solving specific problems and recognizing marketing opportunities. Typical examples of such problems are the need to launch a new product, a new competitor entering the marketplace, or a decline in sales volume. For example, a publisher might experience a drop in sales volume of undergraduate texts; they would wish to investigate the cause of such a decline. Marketing research specifies the information necessary to investigate the situation, designs the methods for collecting the data, analyses and interprets the data, and communicates the findings. The information that is collected is not otherwise available to the organization or, in other words, cannot be collected through marketing information systems.

**Marketing information systems** are the framework for the day-to-day management and structuring of information gathered regularly from sources both

155

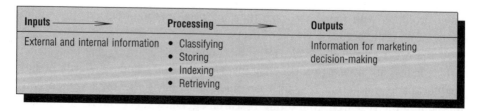

**Figure 9.1** A marketing information system

inside and outside an organization. They encompass processes that convert information from a range of sources into information that can support marketing decision-making, as summarized in Figure 9.1. There are a number of different types of marketing information systems that offer varying levels of processing and packaging of the information.

**Marketing knowledge repositories** contain valuable information concerning the marketplace that market research and marketing information systems have collected. This repository, which is part of the wider knowledge repository of the organization, should form the basis of its **marketing intelligence** – the composite of all marketing information and ideas available within an organization, coupled with a perspective on the information that provides a competitive edge.

## MARKETING QUESTIONS AND RESEARCH APPROACHES

A marketing research process will be triggered by a problem. Figure 9.2 lists the types of questions that often form the focus of marketing research activity. The initial problem must be converted into a research question, and then into research objectives. Figure 9.3 illustrates this process. Each stage demands considerable judgement, and understanding of the contexts is required in order to convert a problem statement into a question, and then a research question into research objectives.

The different kinds of problems and research objectives give rise to different types of studies. These are as follows:

- **Exploratory studies** generate preliminary data to help to clarify or define a problem and identify issues and directions for further research. They provide the initial assessment, which supports the planning of more formal research. Typical questions that might be explored through an exploratory study include: What new products might be of interest? How can we increase footfall in the library? Are subject gateways providing the right kind of navigational support?
- **Descriptive studies** describe market or customer characteristics, and

**Who**

- are our customers?
- should our customers be?
- are our competitors?

**What**

- new/existing products and services should we develop?
- new/existing markets should we enter?

**Where**

- should we develop?
- are our customers?
- should we distribute our products and services?
- are our competitors?

**When**

- should we launch new products and services?
- should we enter new/leave existing markets?

**How**

- should we promote our products and services?
- should we distribute our products and services?
- should we handle consumer reactions/expectations?
- should we compete?
- should we maintain our performance and evaluate new opportunities?

**Why**

- should consumers buy our products and services?
- should we develop new products and services?
- should we remain in particular markets/businesses?

*Source:* Beaumont (1991).

**Figure 9.2** Fundamental marketing questions

- Problem statement: Decline in the sales of undergraduate texts
- Research questions: What is the cause of the decline in the sales of undergraduate texts? What strategies can be adopted to reverse this decline, or should the publisher's efforts be directed to other markets?
- Research objectives: To identify the market segments (on the basis of subject and library vs consumer) in which the decline has occurred To collect data from those segments which offer insights into the reasons for the decline

**Figure 9.3** Developing research objectives

157

thereby provide the marketer with a better understanding of a particular issue or problem. They may be used to profile customers, or to assess their relationship (in both attitudinal and behavioural terms) with the organization. Descriptive studies often involve a large-scale survey.

- **Causal studies** seek to investigate the effect of one variable on another, to establish a cause and effect relationship between two variables. Organizations might, for example, be interested to assess whether there is any relationship between an increase in a promotional budget and sales volume, and to be able to identify the nature of that relationship. In practice, such relationships are difficult to establish, because in the real world there are usually too many other variable factors that may cloud the relationship between the two variables under examination.

Research can also be divided into two groups on the basis of whether it is qualitative or quantitative in nature:

- **Qualitative research** involves the collection of data that are open to interpretation, for example in investigating motivation, attitudes and beliefs, and intentions. It is often based on small-scale samples and cannot be statistically generalized. The results are often subjective, tentative and impressionistic, but qualitative research may offer a depth of insight into complex situations that would be difficult to achieve with quantitative research. Qualitative research helps in understanding the factors that influence consumer attitudes and behaviour, and can therefore be useful in the design phase of a qualitative study, or as a basis for projections about future actions and reactions.
- **Quantitative research** involves the collection of data that are quantifiable, such as sales figures, demographic information, market share, market size, number and type of customer complaints, number of help-desk enquiries handled. Quantitative research requires a representative sample that is sufficiently large that the researcher can be confident that results can be generalized to apply to the wider population. Market research agencies conduct a number of specialized continuous surveys on behalf of retailers and manufacturers. These include syndicated surveys of retail purchases, consumer panels, home audits (of groceries purchased), and omnibus surveys (which collect data on a range of topics for a number of organizations). These agencies have a range of very sophisticated ways of collecting data, and are increasingly capturing these data at the point of the event, using various computer-aided data entry approaches.

## COLLECTING DATA

There are two types of data that might be collected in market research: primary and secondary.

- **Primary data** are those that are observed and recorded or collected directly from respondents. Primary data collection, or field research, is undertaken by or commissioned by an organization for a specific purpose. The required information does not already exist, so that it needs to be collected, usually from customers and potential customers. The advantage of primary data is that they should be tailored to the problem in hand, but they can be expensive and time-consuming to collect.
- **Secondary data** are those that have already been compiled inside or outside the organization for some purpose other than the current investigation. Secondary data, often described as desk research, are much quicker and cheaper to access than field research, and may provide information, such as demographic trends, that the organization may not be in a position to gather. The main role of secondary data is in providing background information on industries and markets.

Figure 9.4 summarizes some of the key methods that can be used in the collection of both primary and secondary data.

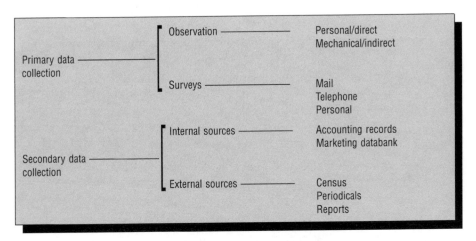

**Figure 9.4** Data collection methods

## SECONDARY DATA COLLECTION

If secondary data exist that can be used to inform further research design or, alternatively, to answer some or all of the research questions, then they should always be used in preference to primary data. For these reasons secondary data collection normally precedes primary data collection. The precise sources to be consulted depend on the nature of the problem. Figure 9.5 illustrates some of the myriad of sources of secondary data. Most of these sources are published; some are available through business libraries, but other specialized sources, such as business and financial databases, may require a special subscription. All sources are updated regularly. Some of these sources provide useful data for publishers and other information providers.

In addition to these sources, data may also be gathered from the following:

1. Management information systems, which provide summary data on the transactions effected within the organization. These data may relate to sales, costs, customer accounts and profits. In the library context, many of these data will be collected in the library management system, but it is important to remember that such data only relate to specified aspects of library and information use. Data logging and records of Website visits will become increasingly important.
2. Syndicated data services can be contracted by client organizations to collect consumer information periodically. Typically, they may circulate market

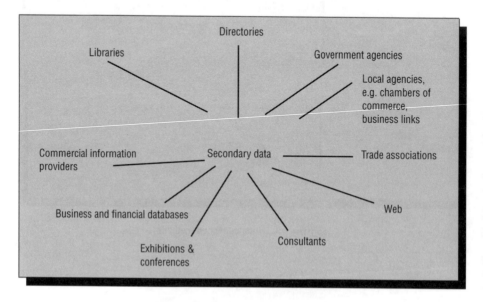

**Figure 9.5** Sources of secondary data

research questionnaires that cover a range of products and services from various organizations and feed selected information back. Newspaper publishers use such services, and in the future others in the information marketplace, such as search-engine providers, may find this approach useful. Indeed, there is a future role for online data collection for these services.

3. Demographic analysis, such as is performed by CACI and CCN, may provide customer profiles. There are various sources that profile local communities and these can be useful in the delivery of public services, such as public libraries, or to online information or media providers that are seeking to reach a consumer market.

## PRIMARY DATA COLLECTION

Primary research uses a range of data collection techniques, which gather data from customers or users. The research should be designed to be:

- **valid**, so that the research measures what is required, given the purpose of the project;
- **thorough**, so that the scope of the investigation is appropriate; and
- **reliable and consistent**, so that the same results would arise, with the same test conducted again on subsequent occasions, under the same conditions.

### Sampling

Many populations are so large that it is not possible to interview or collect questionnaires from every member. Most research is therefore based on a subset of the population, described as a sample. There are many ways of selecting a sample; the most appropriate depends on the research objectives. Random or probability sampling is where each member of the population has an equal or known chance of being selected. The advantage of this type of sampling is that it is possible to specify the accuracy with which the sample data can be regarded as representative of the population. Random samples can, however, be difficult to identify. The researcher may not have a complete list of the population from which a sample can be drawn, and even if such a list exists, it may be expensive to contact the members. Telephone interviewing members of a random sample of the users of an online search service might involve problems of language, time zones, and long-distance telephone calls. Non-random sampling is often used, since it is easier and more flexible. Two common approaches are:

- judgmental sampling, in which the individuals to be contacted are specifically selected on the basis of the quality of the information it is perceived they may be able to offer. This approach is common in organizational markets.

The librarian may, for example, talk to managers to get a view on the effectiveness of a current-awareness service to their staff. This might not, of course, provide the whole picture, but it is a useful starting-point;

- quota sampling, which is a convenient means of gathering a sample that reflects the population, but without needing to pursue the individual members of a sampling list.

There is a range of survey methods; the selection of an appropriate one depends upon the nature of the problem, the data needed, and the resources available. Below we briefly discuss some of the more common approaches: interviews; focus groups; observation; and questionnaires. Brief mention is then made of prototyping and experiments. Practical tips on choosing respondents are given in Figure 9.6.

**Individual interviews**   Interviews are useful for gathering facts and opinions; the data collected are generally qualitative. The two-way communication that is a feature of interviews should provide a more multidimensional analysis of the situation, yielding qualitative data concerning not only what a user does, but also why they do it.

There are two main types of one-to-one interview: **structured interviews** and **unstructured or flexible interviews**, sometimes called **in-depth interviews**. Structured interviews are guided by a set of predetermined questions, often recorded on an interview checklist. These are easier to analyse, and comparing the comments made by different people is more straightforward. Flexible interviews are guided only by a list of set topics; the interviewer allows the interview to develop in response to the interviewee's comments. Such interviews are useful for 'discovering the unknown' and identifying facts or attitudes that might not have been predicted to be an issue, and therefore might be omitted from a more structured interview based on a predetermined checklist. The main disadvantages of this type of interview are that they are time-consuming, need to be conducted by a trained interviewer, and can consequently be very

1. Define the nature, size and characteristics of the group to be surveyed.
2. Consider the research objectives, in terms of whether the research is exploratory, descriptive, or causal.
3. Decide whether the research design needs to be qualitative or quantitative.
4. Identify a sampling frame (list of the members of the population). If this is not available, consider non-random approaches to gathering a sample that is likely to yield insights into the problem.
5. Select a sampling method, taking into account the balance between the need for representativeness, accessibility and convenience.

**Figure 9.6** Practical tips on choosing respondents

expensive. **Semi-structured interviews** are guided by a list of topics, but the way in which this list is used depends upon the interviewee's responses; accordingly, the interview may progress along different routes.

**Focus groups**   Focus groups are group discussions with, say, eight to ten people, specially selected in accordance with a set of predetermined criteria. The members of the group exchange attitudes, experiences and beliefs about the particular topic. The advantages of focus groups are:

- respondents experience a sense of safety in numbers and therefore greater willingness to express insights and greater spontaneity;
- the process highlights the possible range of different attitudes and behaviours in a relatively short time;
- the group can be observed with the aim of yielding data on reactions, vocabulary and perceptions;
- group discussion triggers counter-responses, which might not surface in individual discussion.

The disadvantages of focus groups are that:

- they may inhibit frank and confidential exchanges on sensitive issues;
- minority viewpoints and less dominant personalities may be lost;
- group leadership and facilitation requires training and expertise.

REFLECT: How might a school library use focus groups not only to encourage the use of the service, but also better to understand why the service is not being used as much as it could be?

**Questionnaires and surveys**   Questionnaires can be used either to conduct a wider survey than might be possible with other methods, or to collect subjective data, such as user attitudes that customers might not be prepared to discuss in a person-to-person situation. If users are scattered and it is impossible to conduct interviews, a questionnaire may elicit a quick response from a large number of people. Questionnaires may also be used to identify 'key' individuals, so that interviews can be focused on these individuals. They provide quantitative data, which means that analysis is likely to involve at least some basic statistical processing. The nature of these analyses must be determined at the questionnaire design stage, and not after the data have been collected.

Questionnaire design is a skilled activity, and the development of an appropriate format may take a considerable period of time. Several drafts, followed by pilot trials, may be necessary.

Questions can be **closed** or **open**. Closed questions, which list the range of potential answers, tend to reduce ambiguity and misinterpretation and are quicker to answer and analyse. They are often preferred but their effective use depends critically upon the appropriate selection of questions and potential answers. Open questions are useful where the range of possible responses cannot be readily predicted, and here they can assist in collecting ideas.

Questionnaires may be used in:

- **postal surveys,** in which respondents are requested to complete and return a questionnaire through the post. Non-response is a big concern with these. The advantages lie in the ease with which confidentiality can be maintained and the absence of interviewer bias. Postal questionnaires are also a reasonably cheap means of gathering feedback from a relatively large number of people;
- **telephone surveys** use a questionnaire as a basis for a telephone interview. These surveys are more flexible than postal surveys and can use semi-structured questions, but require an input of interviewer time and skill.

Once questionnaires have been completed and returned to the researcher, any rating scales are converted to numerical values and appropriate statistical analysis is performed. Typically this may involve the calculation of descriptive statistics such as means and standard deviations, and cross-tabulations. More sophisticated analysis, possibly using multivariate analysis, will be necessary for surveys including members from a number of different market segments, and where one proposed outcome is a profile of the differences between such segments.

*REFLECT: What are the limitations of e-mail questionnaires in collecting opinions on the effectiveness of a short loan service in an academic library?*

**Observation**   Trained observers watch particular individuals or groups, such as customers, potential customers, children, or information systems users. The objective is to gather information on some aspect of consumer behaviour and reaction. Observation is not as straightforward as it may seem, since observers bring a host of preconceptions to the observation process; cross-checking analysis based on observation is important, and can be performed by using other research methods, or by other observers conducting parallel observations.

In **direct observation** users are observed in specific environments, possibly fulfilling specific tasks. They may be offered a new type of information product to investigate, or they may be asked to use a new piece of electronic equipment. Cognitive information such as attitudes, beliefs, motivations and perceptions cannot be observed. One way of gathering this information is **active observation**, where the subject is asked about their actions after the observation episode. Such discussions are also an option with **indirect observation**, in which a video-recording of the subject is made, and the subject and the observer then discuss the recording. These approaches have been used in usability testing of new interface designs, such as Web pages, and are useful in testing the acceptability of the design of new information products. In organizational marketing contexts, observation or behaviour at exhibitions may reveal insights into customer responses to the promotional activities and products of the organization and its competitors. Subjectivity, and the likelihood that a subject who is aware that they are being watched may modify their behaviour, are the key limitations of observation.

**Experiments** Experiments are normally conducted in laboratory environments in which it is possible to manipulate some of the variables and hold others constant, and determine the effect of changing aspects of a design for promotion purposes, or aspects of a product. An experiment might, for example, be used to investigate how a group of students makes use of a subject information portal. Because well-designed experiments involve careful control of most variables so that other variables can be isolated, most experiments have a very narrow scope, and are of limited applicability. **Walk-throughs** are a type of field experiment useful for assessing service experiences, whether they be real or virtual. In designing a walk-through an expert determines the exact task, context and important characteristics of the user population. The evaluator then 'walks through' the necessary action or tasks that take users towards their likely goals with a view to identifying the problems likely to be encountered and strategies used to solve them. Walk-throughs are widely used in testing the functionality of new information systems; their use in a service context was discussed in Chapter 4.

**Prototyping** Prototyping is mainly used in the development of information products, rather than specifically in relation to other aspects of the marketing mix. It merits brief mention in this context, since it is an approach that encourages collaboration in the product design process. The customer (or sometimes experts as representatives of customer groups) and the producer work in partnership to produce a product that meets the needs of the user. The producer first produces a prototype, or the best product that they can on the basis of the available specification. The potential customer then evaluates this prototype and makes suggestions for improvement, many of which will then be incorporated into the final product. Customer response Beta testing is a type of market testing that is common with new software and other information products where it may be difficult to assess in advance whether the product matches customer needs.

## CONCLUDING MARKETING RESEARCH

Data collection must be planned so that the data can be easily fed into a data analysis process. The best collection methods are those where the subject enters the data in a form that is automatically fed into the data analysis software, such as online questionnaires, or questionnaires using optical marks that can be scanned for data entry. Thus an academic library customer satisfaction questionnaire that allows students to express their opinions through an online questionnaire, and then transmits the data straight to a database for statistical analysis, is a very efficient method. Such an approach is particularly useful with surveys that are conducted on a regular basis. Approaches to data analysis should be planned early in the research process. Appropriate data analysis depends on the hypothesis or question, and whether the data collected are qualitative or quantitative. Quantitative data analysis will need to create data tabulation and associated statistical interpretations using both descriptive and summary statistics such as means and standard deviations, and multivariate analysis and hypothesis testing. Qualitative and quantitative analysis of significant data sets is extremely time-consuming. There is a range of computer-based tools, such as content analysis and statistical analysis packages, that can support these processes.

Research findings must be recorded in a form that is appropriate for their audience. Managers benefit from executive summaries and other lists of key points. Finally, all research findings have limitations. Acknowledgement of these limitations is important in the interpretation of the results. It may also serve to identify areas for further research or investigation. Practical tips for conducting a marketing research exercise are given in Figure 9.7.

## MARKETING INFORMATION SYSTEMS

Marketing information systems (MKIS) must be designed to support the types of decision-making in which marketers need to engage. Information comes in a variety of forms and from a variety of sources. The problem is to extract relevant information, or information that might become relevant in the future, and to make it accessible to those managers who might find it useful. Most organizations are drowning in information. As well as generating huge amounts of data from their day-to-day transactions (sales, customer details, incoming and outgoing orders), organizations are usually gathering information about competitors, and all the STEP (see Chapter 2) influences on the marketing environment. It is the role of the marketing information system to collect and organize these data. The information gathered comes from both internal and external sources.

1. Define the problem that has triggered the need for a marketing research exercise.
2. Interpret the problem definition into one or more research questions, and from these develop research objectives. Keep these to the point.
3. Plan the research, using, as necessary:
   - a **research brief**, which can act as a basis for discussion between the manager with the problem and the marketing research team. This should specify the problem, research objectives, timescales, budget and reporting requirements;
   - a **research plan**, which records the agreement on the details of the research project. Typically this might cover: objectives; research methods; data analysis to be performed; responsibilities and personnel; data ownership; reporting arrangements; format of the final report; and schedules and budgets.
4. Collect the data, including:
   - secondary data, to ensure a good understanding of the context and to inform any primary data collection;
   - primary data collection, including the design of any data collection tools, such as interview schedules, pilot studies, and the main study. Keep the tools as simple as possible.
5. Analyse and interpret information (and realize that you have collected too much data!), including:
   - quantitative data – analysis using software tools with a range of statistical techniques;
   - qualitative data – if necessary transcribe interview recordings and perform content analysis.
6. Prepare and present the report. Typical contents include: title; contents page; executive summary; introduction; research methods; findings; discussion of findings; conclusions; recommendations; and (carefully selected) appendices.
7. Evaluate research. Although this is always necessary, it is particularly important for annual and other regular surveys in which similar approaches may be used again.

**Figure 9.7**  Practical tips on conducting a marketing research exercise

The former include sales records, marketing research reports, sales representatives reports, customer enquiries and complaints. For retailers, and other service points, such as libraries, systems which identify customers and items using bar codes at the point of transaction have generated important potential for collecting information about stock movement and customer activities. External sources include *ad hoc* market research studies, information from all the sources in Figure 9.5, and also continuous input from syndicated studies, market research agencies, suppliers, partners and business and financial database providers.

Figure 9.2 listed some generic marketing questions. Using one of these questions as an example may help to illustrate the different types of data that are needed in a marketing information system. The question 'Where are our customers?' requires data to be collected on two levels. Data collected from existing customers, including characteristics such as age, family groupings, distance travelled to the store and buying behaviour, will yield a profile of existing customers. Potential customers can be located by using this profile and matching it against external demographic data to identify the location of other members of the public with a profile similar to that of existing customers.

167

*REFLECT: What information does your organization give to its suppliers,*
*which might be used as input to their MKIS?*

MKIS, like all other types of information systems, can be broadly categorized into four kinds: transaction and operational data processing systems; management information systems; decision support systems; and executive information systems. These categories reflect the different levels at which marketing information is collected and analysed. The types of data embedded in such systems and the range of reports and queries that they can be expected to generate offer a further insight into the kinds of questions MKIS must be able to answer. The categories are outlined below:

1. Transaction and operational data processing systems maintain records concerning the basic operations of the business. Examples include library management systems, sales transactions and inventory systems. Such systems may assist the service agent in responding to individual customers, and in customizing the service encounter.
2. Management information systems (MIS) often make use of the data in transaction processing systems, but offer basic summaries and analyses of those data. Typical outputs from MIS are structured, scheduled, and/or exception reports on branch sales by product line, with associated exception reports highlighting important conditions such as below-average branch sales. They assist managers in ensuring that products are available to match customer demand. Library management systems generate details of user demand for books or electronic documents on a regular basis by, say, branch, collection or subject area. In a lifelong learning project, it may be necessary to design a data collection and analysis procedure to monitor and report on the impact of a project within the community.
3. Decision support systems (DSS) assist managers with unique, non-recurring strategic decisions that are relatively unstructured. DSS use a database management system to store data, and a model-building and data analysis facility to allow the building of models that describe the interrelationships between the important variables in a particular environment. A good example of a DSS that might be used in marketing is a geographical information system. One widespread application of GIS is in retail locational planning, but GIS is also used to support decisions about the location of public service delivery points. DSS, in general, assists senior managers to make decisions in relation to new products, new service delivery locations and messages and audiences for promotion and brand images. They gather and present data to guide decisions about major new initiatives.
4. Executive information systems (EIS) are designed to assist top-level executives with the acquisition and use of the information that is necessary for

strategic management. The emphasis is on presentation and ease of use in highly unstructured decision situations which need to draw on information from a wide range of sources. For example, a manager may wish to compare last year's sales figures with those of a competitor. To do this, the manager accesses reports on publicly held companies which are available from external financial databases and then finds the yearly sales figures for the manager's own organization. The EIS will compare, in graphical form, the competitor's sales with the organization's sales. An EIS would be a valuable tool for a publisher that wanted to monitor its success in electronic and traditional marketplaces, and to compare sales and revenue figures with those of other publishers, and trends in the marketplace as a whole.

In recent years technological opportunities for the collection of data about customers and their activities have affected the role and nature of marketing information systems. For example, loyalty cards have been introduced by a number of retailers. These usually allow customers to collect points which are recorded on the magnetic strip on the back of the card, together with the details of the items purchased. When a customer has collected a certain number of points, they can collect a gift. Loyalty cards provide retailers with information on individuals' weekly purchases and how product associations are being made. The effectiveness of promotions can also be analysed by the number of items on offer sold (Gonzalez, 1997). Every time a loyalty card is swiped at the point of sale, the retailer's systems are triggered to record the name of the shopper, the time that they came to shop, the store that they visited and the entire content of their trolley (Field, 1997). Library registration cards could and should be reconceptualized as loyalty cards.

*REFLECT: How could library registration cards be used to help to build a relationship with library users?*

E-shopping, like loyalty cards, offers a valuable opportunity to collect information about a customer. Online customer registration can gather basic personal details, such as name, address, age, marital status and sex. Each order provides additional information concerning the purchase transactions that an individual chooses to make. This allows a provider to create a profile of individual customers' purchasing behaviour, and then generate management data by summarizing the purchasing behaviour of a number of individuals across a range of products. Many such transactions relate to the delivery or purchase of information products. The opportunities for profiling customers in the information marketplace are significant, provided that the marketer knows the questions to which they need answers.

## CONCLUSION

> The future is in delivering information about customers to all the parts where customers interact with retailers. It's about staff at the checkout, the counter and the call centre knowing enough about the customer to be able to give a personal, courteous service. And it's about being able to identify the customer when they get in touch via the Internet or kiosk. (Field, 1997, p. 46)

This vision will not be achieved without a greater appreciation of the questions that businesses need to ask concerning their customers and their purchasing habits. Such approaches are important in 'knowing your customers'.

Marketing research projects are useful in collecting data to solve specific problems, and to accommodate changes in product range, customer profile and the marketing environment. Data from such studies should be integrated with information generated from the analysis of the organization's activities and other internal and external sources of information.

## REFERENCES AND FURTHER READING

Beaumont, J.R. (1991), 'GIS and market analysis', in Maguire, D.J., Goodchild, M.F. and Rhind, D.W. (eds), *Geographical Information Systems: Principles and Applications*. London: Longman, pp. 139–51.

Chisnall, P.M. (1986), *Marketing Research*. 3rd edition. London: McGraw-Hill.

Clarke, I. and Rowley, J.E. (1995), 'GIS and DSS in strategic retail locational planning', *International Journal of Retail and Distribution Management*, **23** (3), 4–10.

Field, C. (1997), 'Data goes to market – utilising information obtained from loyalty cards', *Computer Weekly*, 16 January, pp. 44–6.

Gonzalez, F. (1997), 'Getting to know you (the use of loyalty cards as a direct marketing tool)', *Grocer*, August, **220** (7316), 33.

Hague, P. (1992), *The Industrial Market Research Handbook*. 3rd edition. Kogan Page.

Hewitt, M. (1998), 'Loyalty's limits', *Marketing*, 29 January, 16–18.

Jenkinson, A. (1995), 'Retailing and shopping on the Internet', *International Journal of Retail and Distribution Management*, **24** (3), 26–37.

Piercy, N. and Evans, M. (1983), *Managing Marketing Information*. London: Croom Helm.

Rowley, J.E. (1998), 'Internet food retailing: the UK context', *British Food Journal*, **100** (2), 85–95.

Rowley, J.E. and Peacefull, L.G. (1995), 'A Review of geographic information systems in the United Kingdom', *Information Services and Use*, **15**, 103–15.

# 10 Marketing strategy and planning

## AIMS

This chapter draws together the range of operational marketing concerns that have been explored earlier in this text. Specifically it:

- differentiates between corporate strategy, marketing strategy and marketing planning;
- explores some of the models used in marketing strategy and analysis to understand the competitive position in marketplaces; and
- reviews the stages in the marketing planning process.

The chapter aims to encourage information professionals to think about the context in which they are operating, to plan and to take a longer-term perspective.

## INTRODUCTION

This book has explored the practical elements of marketing as embedded in the marketing mix, and has introduced the tools for implementation of the marketing concept. But so far, the focus on the marketing mix elements has been largely operational, and directed on the short term. These operational considerations must be placed in the context of a wider strategic perspective, which explores the answers to questions such as:

- Which markets should we be in?
- What can our organization offer that is distinct from that offered by competitors or even collaborative partners?
- Does the organization have the skills, resources and other assets necessary to achieve its objectives?

171

- How will our marketplace position change over the next five years?
- What will our competitors be doing in five years?
- What benefits will our customers expect in five years?

Strategic concerns affect the entire organization, and form the framework for future operational decisions and planning. Whilst the questions above might appear to be simple, answering them is often far from straightforward. Good information from marketing research and marketing information systems as discussed in Chapter 9 is an important basis for forecasting. Nevertheless, trends in the marketplace can be difficult to foresee, and it may be even more difficult to predict their long-term effect. Strategic planning takes place against a backdrop of risk and uncertainty.

Marketing strategy is closely intertwined with corporate strategy and marketing planning, and it can be difficult to discern the differences between these processes and their associated documents. This chapter therefore begins with some definitions.

- **Corporate strategy** is concerned with the allocation of resources within the organization in order to achieve the business direction and scope consistent with corporate objectives. It specifies the organization's mission, defines organizational objectives, and identifies the portfolio of activities for the organization. Typical issues of concern to corporate planners are: market expansion; product development; acquisition; divestment; diversification; and maintaining a competitive edge. These are all issues that affect the market segments and product ranges with which the organization is involved. It is not surprising, then, that in a customer-focused organization there is a dynamic relationship between the corporate strategy and the marketing strategy.
- The **marketing strategy** of an organization indicates the specific markets towards which activities are to be targeted, and the types of competitive advantages that are to be developed and exploited. It may be concerned with issues such as customers and customer relationships, and the establishment of appropriate marketing mix strategies.
- **Marketing planning** focuses on the operational detail, converting strategies into implementable actions. It is a detailed statement, which specifies target markets, marketing programmes, responsibilities, timescales, resources to be used, and budgets. Marketing strategy considers all aspects of an organization's strategy in the marketplace, whilst a marketing plan is more usually focused on implementing marketing and promotional strategies in the context of specific target markets and the marketing mix.

Organizations may develop both a marketing strategy and a marketing plan, or produce a plan that is an amalgamation of the two. Different models will be appropriate for different organizations. The most effective approach will be influenced by the size of the organization, the scale of its marketing activity, the strategic planning process, market structure and opportunities, and the extent of the marketing orientation of the organization.

*REFLECT: Locate examples of planning documents relating to marketing in an organization known to you. What is their scope and coverage?*

## MARKETING STRATEGY AND ANALYSIS

Marketing strategies are formulated by organizations with the objective of improving their competitive position, usually through developing a competitive advantage. The global objective of the marketing strategy for any organization is that it moves as far as possible from the conditions that underpin perfect competition; in other words, the organization must seek to differentiate itself from its competitors, either in reality or in the perception of its customers. In order to achieve this it needs to be aware of the nature of the marketplace, and specifically its competitors. Before an organization can formulate an effective long-term strategy, it must understand and profile its competitors' current activities, and have a sufficient appreciation of their strengths and weaknesses to be able to predict, with some accuracy, their likely future actions in terms of product innovation, entry to new marketplaces, strategic alliances, mergers and acquisitions. In the public sector, political agendas, government proposals and priorities are important in influencing the initiatives taken by all organizations in the marketplace and the creation of new government organizations. For example, the agencies responsible for providing information and advice to businesses in the United Kingdom have been restructured and renamed many times in recent years.

Marketing thinkers have proposed a number of models that are useful in analysing industries and their players. First we explore approaches that consider the structure of industries and marketplaces, and then competitor analysis, which focuses on the strengths and weaknesses of individual competitors.

Different industries and sectors have different sources of advantage. Organizations need to be able to understand the basis upon which competitive advantage can be achieved in their own sector and, in particular, to distinguish between those factors that are *expected* in any one sector, as opposed to those that can offer an advantage. One of the challenges arising from advantage based on technological innovation is that the advantage will be short-lived. For example, whilst loyalty cards briefly served to differentiate retailers, they have become the norm, and any differentiation must be based on the advantages that loyalty cards offer customers, or competitive advantage derived from other aspects of the offering. In general, for information products, technological innovation as in, for example, issues of compatibility and use of standard protocols, is a prerequisite rather than a source of competitive advantage. Competitive advantage is more likely to arise from price, customer relationships, quality, or speed of delivery.

A number of models seek to support thinking about marketing strategy, and to make proposals concerning the way in which an organization develops a competitive advantage in the marketplace. These models can be applied to the analysis of your own organization, or to the analysis of competitors' strategies. Here we first explore three such models that focus on the nature and structure of the industry:

- Porter's model of competitive forces
- Porter's comparative advantage model
- Cost-structure-based marketing strategy.

These models are just a selection of those available. Together they offer some perspectives on the nature of competitive advantage. Next, we briefly consider the issue of competitor analysis through the medium of the Boston Matrix. The purpose of such models is to clarify thinking about industry structures, competitors and marketing strategies. They provide starting-points, and may be useful in seminars and group discussions that seek to draw out a shared understanding among a group of managers or professionals so that visions and futures can be formulated. If one model does not provide useful insights, then a different model can be tried.

## PORTER'S MODEL OF COMPETITIVE FORCES

Porter (1980) developed a model that summarizes the key factors that affect industry attractiveness. This model shows the competitive forces at work in an industry. A review of these factors allows organizations to assess to what extent an organization can do better than, or create a competitive advantage over, its rivals. Each of the five forces in Porter's model identifies factors that move an industry closer to perfect competition (in which it is impossible for organizations to achieve competitive advantage), or further away from perfect competition. These five forces are elaborated below and shown in Figure 10.1.

### Power of customers

Powerful customers, such as are often active in business-to-business markets, will be able to demand attractive terms. In the information industry such cus-

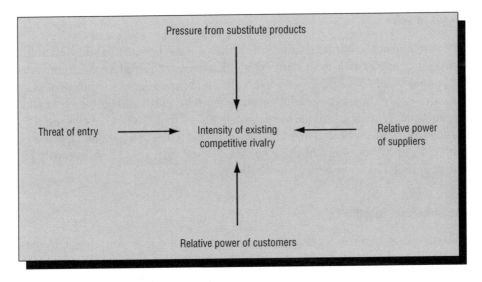

**Figure 10.1** Porter's model of competitive forces

tomers may be consortia of libraries or higher education institutions. On the other hand, if the product is much more important to the purchaser than to the producer, the producer has considerable freedom in the nature and terms of the product offering. This is the case if there are few substitutes, or where there is a monopoly. Many public services, such as health, education and social services, fall into this category, in which the direct power of customers is weak.

### Power of suppliers

In markets in which the producer can credibly threaten to make its own components, or to cut out distributors and sell directly to end-users, its bargaining power is strong when contracting with suppliers and distributors. Technological innovation, such as CD-ROM, has seen database publishers who might previously have supplied to the end-customer through, say, an online search service develop direct contacts with suppliers. The Web offers all businesses, including those selling information products, new opportunities to eliminate steps in the supply chain. An important source of power is the additional customer and purchase information that the 'retailer' can glean from e-business transactions, both through the Web and at service points in libraries and supermarkets.

### Threat of entry

The threat of entry will be significantly reduced if the barriers to entry are high. Barriers to entry arise from both economic factors and product differentiation. Economic factors determine potential profits, and include any economies of scale that are achieved by large producers and their differential ability to raise capital. Product differentiation will be based on the ability to deliver benefits sought by customers. In the information marketplace, barriers to entry are often associated with the difficulties of establishing the intellectual capacity and skills needed in the generation of knowledge. Knowledge is a key asset.

### Pressure from substitutes

Products that represent unique packages of benefits that are sought by customers are least vulnerable to substitution. In general, challenges from substitutes take the form of sideways competition, which offers an alternative means of providing the same benefit. Rapid change in technological marketplaces has meant that there has been and will continue to be a range of ways in which users can access information. Electronic information can be seen as a substitute for print information, although these alternative media do not offer exactly the same benefits. Technological advances such as electronic books and electronic encyclopedias are designed to offer all the benefits of the print equivalent, with additional benefits, such as multimedia inserts or the ability to cut and paste sections of the document, and thereby erode the marketplace for the print equivalent. Whether a product should be regarded as a substitute for another product ultimately depends on the bundles of benefits that are sought by customers; it is also important to remember that the availability of new products may shift customers' perceptions about the benefits that they seek.

### Intensity of rivalry

The other four forces influence the intensity of rivalry in an industry. In addition, other factors also have an effect. The key issue in rivalry is how important it is for companies to make a sale or sign a contract. This may be determined to a considerable extent by whether the industry carries significant fixed costs, which need to be covered. This means that companies are often prepared to sell on a marginal costing basis during demand downswings, and competition will be fierce. Such competition is common in service suppliers such as those in the airline and hotel industries, where seats and rooms, respectively, must be filled. It is also likely to be encountered in any competitive context in the information industry for two reasons. First, where an information service is being provided, and staff are made available to provide that service (as in libraries or call centres), capacity will be determined in advance, and an organization will be keen to achieve that capacity either for reasons of profit or, in the public sector, the maximization of utilization of committed resource. In addition, as discussed in Chapter 5, the costs of creating information are associated with the creation of the first copy. Pricing strategies will assume a specified level of sales, which information generators will be keen to achieve.

*REFLECT: Use Porter's five forces model to identify some of the forces in the information marketplace that might affect the Royal College of Nursing Library.*

## PORTER'S COMPARATIVE ADVANTAGE MODEL

Organizations must adapt their marketing strategies in order to maximize their competitive advantage within their particular competitive environment. There are a number of different strategies that they can adopt. Porter proposes a simple model, which is useful in considering the factors that affect marketing strategy. He suggests that there are two key strategies that organizations can use as a basis for creating a competitive advantage:

- differentiation, or
- cost leadership.

**Differentiation** is concerned with identifying and delivering a product benefit or bundle of benefits that customers seek. Sources of differentiation can arise from any area of the market offering, including product, branding, price, place, promotion, and service quality and people. Figure 10.2 lists some of the approaches to achieving differentiation.

- Create or reinforce non-cost-based barriers to market entry, such as government regulations, or import and export controls.
- Pursue strong branding.
- Employ a highly specialized or skilled sales force, who perhaps have expertise in installing computer networks, which they share with customers.
- Dominate a niche market.
- Possess or cultivate specialist knowledge or technology, such as buyers, craft skills or chief executives who can spot a trend (or subject librarians who are up to date with the latest business information sources).
- Invest in intellectual property and protect that investment through patents and designs.
- Pursue exclusivity in links to a distribution network, or in other strategic alliances.

**Figure 10.2** Approaches to achieving comparative advantage by differentiation

*REFLECT: Review the options for achieving differentiation in Figure 10.2. Which of these are options in your organization?*

**Cost leadership** is achieved by exercising tight control over production and distribution costs. This is normally achieved through one of the following:

- Economies of scale, which allow fixed costs to be spread over several units. For economies of scale to have a significant impact they must be effected in an important part of the value chain.
- Accumulation of experience, which leads to the development of more cost-efficient production and distribution methods.
- Superior technology.
- Operational logistics, where, for example, feedback on actual sales levels can trigger additional production.

A key limitation of cost leadership strategies is that there is only one cost leader in any one marketplace, whereas differentiation allows a number of organizations to differentiate themselves in unique ways. However, the benefits achieved through cost leadership can be used as a basis for differentiation on the basis of price, position or support.

These key dimensions of differentiation and cost leadership have been used in the comparative advantage model. This model can either be used to note the link between optimum strategies in different marketplaces, or to profile different marketplaces. For example, we might argue that in a market in which there are a few large players, organizations will need to exhibit both cost leadership and differentiation strategies. Figure 10.3 shows how marketing strategies can be identified on the basis of this model. Importantly, strategies should differ according to the role that the organization expects to play in the marketplace.

In practice, many organizations exhibit combinations of cost leadership and differentiation. Nevertheless, the model can be useful in starting to analyse a marketplace. In addition, it may yield some insight into the marketing strategies

| | | Cost leadership | |
|---|---|---|---|
| | | *Yes/high* | *No/low* |
| **Differentiation** | *Yes/high* | A few large players, each focused on a particular market segment | Many small specialists, probably all making reasonable returns |
| | *No/low* | Trend towards a monopoly supplier | Perfect competition and low overall returns |

**Figure 10.3** The comparative advantage model and industry structures

that different competitors are likely to develop and, further, the marketing strategies that are likely to be successful in the particular industry sector. Figure 10.4 summarizes some of the strategies that are suggested by the comparative advantage model.

**a. strategies for industry leaders**

| | | Scope for cost leadership | |
|---|---|---|---|
| | | *High* | *Low* |
| **Scope for differentiation** | *High* | • Research/invest/specialize<br>• Use cash flow from cost advantage to squash threat of entry | • Research/invest/specialize<br>• Extensive client contact and focus |
| | *Low* | • Add differentiated products with common scale economies to core products<br>• Use cash to squash threats of entry | • Try to transform industry ground rules by seeking ways to gain cost leadership or specialist skills; if impossible then sell business and exit industry |

**b. Strategies for others**

| | | Scope for cost leadership | |
|---|---|---|---|
| | | *High* | *Low* |
| **Scope for differentiation** | *High* | • Seek to control niche markets where your scale is adequate to enable domination, but which are too small or specialized to tempt entry by market leaders | • There are few disadvantages in being small or a non-leading player in this market. Strategies as per the market leaders: specialize to get close to customers |
| | *Low* | • Exit (since you cannot match the cost leader) or drain cash from the business while ensuring that you do not provoke the market leader | • It is not worth being in this marketplace |

**Figure 10.4** The comparative advantage model and marketing strategies

179

## COST-STRUCTURE-BASED MARKETING STRATEGY

Cost-structure-based marketing strategy focuses on the cost structure of different competitors. Most industries have a traditional cost structure (or balance between fixed and variable costs) that is intrinsic to the nature of the activities they undertake. Cost-structure strategies seek to achieve competitive advantage by shifting from the industry norm. Franchising and subcontracting are two such approaches through which some of the risks and costs (that is, those associated with retailing) are shifted to another organization. In higher education, a distance-learning institution such as the Open University would have a very different cost structure from that associated with a university involved in more traditional modes of student experience. Similarly, public access to information over the Internet has a different cost structure to that associated with delivery through local branch libraries or mobile services. In considering the opportunity for structurally based challenges, it is essential to identify the important costs incurred in the organization and those associated with the business processes of competitors.

## CONDUCTING COMPETITOR ANALYSIS

Competitor analysis is concerned with collecting information on and understanding specific competitors and their marketing strategies. The approaches and models of competitor analysis can also be used to better understand partners and their market position, since this will affect their future contribution to any collaborative venture. The information provided through competitor analysis should help to establish competitive advantage. Industry awareness, as discussed in the previous section, contextualizes understanding of a specific competitor's market position.

One source of information is tactical, relating, for instance, to competitors' product changes, new products, product pricing, levels of discounts and so on. If this information is collated, accessible and kept over a long period of time, it may be possible to discern trends that are useful in interpreting a competitor's marketing strategy.

Strategic marketing intelligence is focused on gaining an understanding of the way in which a competitor is seeking to secure competitive advantage. Specifically, the aim is to identify the competitor's weaknesses, or points of leverage, and thus spot areas in which it is possible to launch a competitive challenge. This involves developing an understanding not only of competitors' current weaknesses, but also making judgements about the options that are open to them. This requires:

• an understanding of the market dynamics and competitive activity;

- an understanding of the constraints that restrict competitors' movement;
- an understanding of competitors' value chains, cost structures and cash flows;
- the evaluation of their strengths and weaknesses with regard to the key success factors in the industry;
- the systematic collection and organization of information;
- the timely analysis of information by senior managers who are in a position to make optimum use of the information in decision-making.

For a large organization, collecting, organizing, interpreting and presenting competitor intelligence is a significant task. A range of business databases and marketing research organizations may also be useful sources of information, and may be accessed through external input into a corporate intranet. See also the practical tips on analysing competitors in Figure 10.5.

A significant factor in competitor analysis is competitor cash flows. This is significantly affected by the rate of growth within specific marketplaces, the relative market share held by a specific product, and the nature of the company's product portfolio. The Boston Consulting Group Matrix is a well-known model which has been used to assist thinking on cash flows in relation to specific products (see Figure 10.6). Given information on relative market shares and industry growth rates, the model can be used to reveal the cash-using or -generating nature of the products produced by two competitors. This model

1. Identify competitors for specific segments in your marketplace. For a large public library offering a wide range of services, competitors will be different for different services. For a document delivery service, customers may have a number of options for obtaining a copy of a journal article. Electronic document delivery services may act as a substitute for more traditional avenues of supply.
2. Find out about their product range, and analyse the difference between your products and theirs. For example, one competitor might be the local video store. What is the difference between the service that they offer and the one that the library offers?
3. Seek to understand the extent of their customer base, in terms of interests, job roles, information needs and geographical coverage.
4. Seek out their strengths and weaknesses, and collect any information on the volume of their activity in different marketplaces, profits and challenges.
5. Seek to understand competitors' objectives. These may be specified in annual reports, public policy statements, Websites and other forms of marketing communication. An understanding of competitor objectives is a significant platform from which to predict their marketing strategy.
6. Note and observe competitors' responses to changes in the marketing environment. Which organizations lead in technological innovation, or in response to public policy change? What does this tell you about their capacity for change, and the significance with which they regard the change?
7. Collect and manage information about competitors with the aid of a competitor information system (as part of a marketing information system).

**Figure 10.5** Practical tips on analysing competitors

| | | Market share (relative to largest competitor) | |
|---|---|---|---|
| | | High | Low |
| **Industry growth** | *High* | Star – eats cash now; makes cash later as growth slows | Question mark – eats cash to grow; cost penalty relative to leader |
| | *Low* | Cash cow – generates cash now; risk of decline later | Dog – uses cash now; little further potential |

**Figure 10.6**  Boston Consulting Group Matrix for analysing product portfolios

only predicts cash flows in industries with significant scale curves and experience effects. These industries are those in which demand evolution follows the conventional lifecycle of cash-hungry fast growth followed by cash-generating stability, where experience gains and scale benefits remain as competitive advantages for the firms that generate them, and where opportunities for product differentiation are limited.

The Boston Matrix assesses products on two dimensions:

1. The level of growth in the product's market. Market growth reflects opportunities and buoyancy in different markets. This is also likely to affect the competitive atmosphere because in high-growth markets there is scope for all players to make gains, whereas in low-growth markets competition is more intense.
2. Market share relative to the largest competitor in the industry.

The Boston Matrix summarizes the market position of the products in an organization's portfolio, and encourages managers to reflect on the current and projected performance of products, and to look at their present and future strategic contribution. The matrix has four categories of product:

1. Dog (low share, low growth) products are likely to be making a loss or a low profit at best, and it is unlikely that the position can be improved. Dogs should only be retained if they are making another strategic contribution other than profit, such as acting as an interface with customers who consequently purchase or use other services or products.
2. Question mark (low share, high growth) products are those that do not appear to be making the impact that might be possible in a high-growth market. Managers need to decide whether further investment in, say, repositioning or promotion would increase the market share, or whether there is a more endemic problem.
3. Star (high share, high growth) products are leaders in a growth market that

demand considerable investment to support further growth and to maintain their lead. Stars have the potential to be the cash cows of the future.

4. Cash cow (high share, low growth) products no longer need the level of support that was necessary for a star, since market growth has slowed and market positions have become relatively entrenched. Managers need to focus on retention and maintenance of market share. Excess cash generated can be used to support other areas.

Some organizations in the information marketplace are not in a position to calculate market growth and relative market share with any precision. This information is often not available in public sector contexts and, further, in the electronic information marketplace rapid growth and frequent changes in products and marketplace structure may make it difficult to generate this type of analysis even for commercial operators. Nevertheless, if used with caution and given careful attention to any assumptions about market growth and relative market share, the matrix can be useful for thinking about the strategic contribution of products in a product portfolio. For organizations with too many market segments, including those in the public sector, and an implied imperative to meet the demands of all of those segments, it may help them to take a more strategic view on their core contributions and lead to more effective prioritization.

*REFLECT: Use the Boston Matrix to analyse the products in your organization's portfolio.*

## COOPERATION AND COLLABORATION

Traditional marketing strategy focuses on businesses that are vying for market position. In order to succeed, they must understand the competition. This allows them to define their position, to fend off attacks on their market from other organizations that are seeking to make inroads into their existing market share, or to launch such an attack themselves. It is not only businesses that are prone to such competitive tactics. Departments within organizations (such as the information management department and the information systems department) and two public sector organizations (such as two libraries in a large urban conurbation) can compete for customers, glory or impact, even when there is no direct profit motive. However, not all competitive behaviour is challenging and confrontational. Many situations are characterized by peaceful coexistence and cooperative alliances. In many marketplaces there is a benign and unwritten agreement that two potential competitors do not invade each other's territory, because there is a risk that such conflict would be damaging for both. Strategic alliances are a more proactive approach to collaboration, in which organizations seek to work together on projects, pooling expertise and resources. Such an alliance may be project-specific or across a number of activities. In the public information sector, EU-funded initiatives and other consortia alliances have been important in encouraging organizations to work together in both horizontal and vertical partnerships. Such alliances have encouraged technological innovation and application that would have been difficult to achieve through other channels, but there are challenges in respect of the long-term commercial position of the products and other outcomes from such initiatives.

*REFLECT: Identify one collaborative venture within the information industry. What have been the benefits for the partners?*

## MARKETING PLANNING

This book has explored the various elements of the marketing mix, and the way in which an organization needs to identify target markets, formulate and develop product offerings and achieve a match between products and the benefits that are sought by members of those markets. This is a dynamic process because the marketing environment changes, competitors and their products may change, and customer needs and preferences are also subject to change. The process of achieving and maintaining a match between product offerings and customer needs requires careful planning and management. Marketing planning, alongside other functional areas of planning within an organization, such as human resource planning and information systems planning, are part of the planning that needs to take place both at an organizational level and within library and information departments. The aim of marketing planning is to ensure that marketing activities are appropriate to the achievement of corporate and unit objectives, can be implemented within resource limits, and are capable of creating and sustaining a competitive position.

One element of marketing planning, the planning of promotional activities, has been discussed in Chapter 7. Promotional planning embraces only one element of the marketing mix, and needs to be conducted and executed in the context of a marketing plan.

Planning is an activity or process that provides a systematic structure and framework for considering the future, appraising opportunities and options, and then selecting and implementing the necessary activities for achieving the stated objectives efficiently and effectively. The marketing plan provides a clear statement of the strategies and actions that will be implemented – by whom, when, and with what outcomes.

Organizations may have a number of different planning processes, resulting in a number of plans. Sometimes these plans are all elements in a corporate system of long-term planning, but on other occasions they may be focused on specific short-term projects or issues. Plans may vary in:

- scope, whether strategic or operational, and functions, products and activities covered;
- timescale, including short-term (around one year or less), medium-term (one to three years), and long-term (three to twenty years);
- regularity – longer-term plans typically have annual cycles to monitor progress and review the plan. A campaign plan might have a limited duration and will be reviewed and evaluated on a timescale appropriate to the activity;
- ownership – marketing plans may be owned at a corporate level, often by a marketing department, or they may be owned by a library or information service. If marketing plans exist at different levels, the relationship between them should be clear, and objectives consistent with each other. When marketing plans are owned by a marketing department, the divide between promotion and other avenues for strengthening customer relationships, such as a responsive customer service, needs special attention.

*REFLECT: What plans does your organization have? Which of these are important for determining the parameters for information marketing planning?*

Whilst planning is essential for success, planning of itself does not guarantee that success. The quality of both the planning process and the outcomes, in the form of the details of the plan, determines success. A plan that no one uses or has read will not inform activities. Staff need the opportunity to contribute to the planning process, need to understand that their performance will be evaluated in terms of their contribution to fulfilling objectives identified in the planning process, and need to be empowered to fulfil their job functions so that they can make an appropriate contribution. Planning must be based on good market information, interpreted using appropriate forecasting techniques. Finally, there should be a recognition that most annual marketing plans will not be executed in their entirety. Management involves making appropriate judgements about modifications to marketing plans as the year progresses, without sinking into chaos.

# THE MARKETING PLANNING PROCESS

Different models of the marketing planning process will be appropriate for different organizations in the information marketplace, depending on the size of the organization, the nature of its product range, the scale of marketing activity, and the customer profile. However, all organizations need to:

- understand the relationship between corporate objectives and marketing objectives;
- understand the context, resources and constraints which affect the achievement of marketing objectives;
- formulate a plan which includes a range of marketing actions;
- monitor progress with implementation of the plan, and the effectiveness of the plan and the planning process.

The marketing planning process is designed to ensure a systematic approach to planning. It consists of a number of stages as summarized in Figure 10.7. Each of these is discussed further below. The marketing planning process must be consistent with circumstances. In an organization in which a marketing orientation is expressed largely through service delivery rather than through specific promotional initiatives, the marketing planning process may be almost concurrent with the corporate planning process, provided that the corporate mission has an appropriate focus on customer relationships. Where marketing is a distinct activity, with separate staff and significant budgets, the planning process

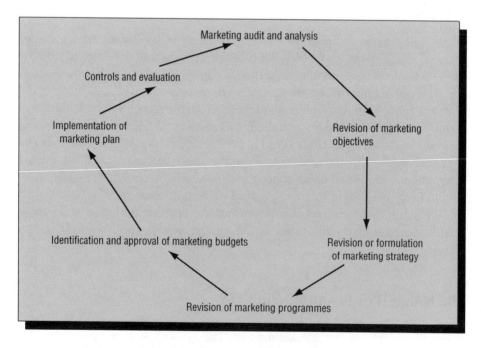

**Figure 10.7**  The marketing planning cycle

will take longer, and will need to specify objectives and proposed actions at a much greater level of detail.

## MARKETING AUDIT AND ANALYSIS

A marketing audit is designed to encourage reflection on the marketplace in which the organization operates and the organization's ability to contribute and respond. Typically it may be focused in terms of questions such as:

1. What is happening in the environment? Does it pose any threats or opportunities?
2. What are our relative strengths and weaknesses in handling and exploiting the environment?
3. How effective are we in implementing marketing activity?

Typically question 1 is the focus of an external audit, which examines the STEP factors discussed in Chapter 2, coupled with competitors' activities and their actual and likely future responses to changes in environmental factors, such as technological and sociocultural changes. Question 2 might be the focus of an internal audit, which focuses on previous performance in relation to aspects of the marketing mix, such as product offering, customer relationships and service quality.

SWOT analysis, otherwise described as an opportunity/issue analysis, is a widely used tool for structuring the information that may be gathered during an audit exercise. It encourages managers to summarize the position in terms of

- Strengths
- Weaknesses
- Opportunities, and
- Threats.

Strengths and weaknesses focus on the present and past, and summarize 'where we are now'. Opportunities and threats encourage consideration of the present and the future, taking a more forward, outward-looking view of future strategic directions. They may summarize 'where we want to be', 'where we do not want to be, but might end up' or 'where we could be if we pursued certain courses of action'. The gap between strengths and weaknesses, and opportunities and threats represents 'what we have to do to get there' and needs to be filled by managerial imagination, inspiration and leadership.

SWOT analysis may be conducted initially in the marketing audit and analysis stage, but reflection on marketing opportunities is intimately associated with the development or review of marketing objectives. SWOT analysis can be used at various stages in the marketing planning cycle, and is a particularly useful tool

1. Formulate a clear view of the service or product for which the SWOT analysis is being conducted.
2. Decide on the time-frame for the future element of the SWOT analysis (e.g. one year or five years).
3. Use a workshop to encourage participation in and ownership of the formulation of the analysis.
4. Recognize that shared and public acknowledgement of weaknesses is difficult and will need support.
5. Encourage a perspective which seeks to transform weaknesses into opportunities.
6. Encourage realistic thinking, with reference to resource issues, about the opportunities that can be grasped.
7. Consider strategies for minimizing threats.

**Figure 10.8** Practical tips on conducting and using a SWOT analysis

in workshops, where it encourages a shared understanding of the organization's successes and failures, and its futures.

Practical tips for conducting and using a SWOT analysis are given in Figure 10.8.

## MARKETING OBJECTIVES

The desire to exploit strengths and opportunities, and to overcome threats and weaknesses, gives a foundation for the definition and review of marketing objectives, which must be formulated in the context of corporate objectives and mission statements. Figure 10.9 gives some examples of marketing objectives. Any attempt to formulate marketing objectives in the absence of such a strategic

**(a) for a subject gateway**
1. To increase the number of visits to the site by academic users in the United Kingdom by 50 per cent in the next year.
2. To assure continued funding for the service through convincing stakeholders of the value of the service.
3. To achieve an income of £100,000 through subscription arrangements with users beyond the UK higher education community.

**(b) for a business information service serving the local community**
1. To improve awareness of the library, its services and resources.
2. To improve awareness of the value of business information to people and organizations in the city.
3. To increase the number of users who visit the library to find information for themselves.
4. To encourage greater use of telephone enquiry services.
5. To increase revenue associated with 'business link' services.
6. To be viewed as an integral component of the business community in the city.
7. To ensure that local councillors understand the value of the service to the community.
8. To establish a reputation for a professional and reliable service.

**Figure 10.9** Marketing objectives

position for the organization, whether an independent business in the information marketplace or a public library within the context of a local authority, will fail. Public sector services are often tempted to try to be all things to all people. Focusing on the development of some unique strengths will extend the audience and visibility beyond immediate publics and users. In an information world in which roles are being redefined and barriers between roles are changing, this approach is a foundation for a more secure future.

Marketing objectives need to link closely with corporate objectives, and also with promotional objectives. They state what is to be achieved through the marketing activity proposed in the plan, and usually relate to one or more of:

- achieving increased or maintaining market share;
- maintaining or improving profitability;
- establishing a position in a new marketplace;
- maximizing cash flow.

Objectives should meet the criteria for SMART objectives. That is, they should be:

- **S**pecific, or focused, giving details of products and market segments
- **M**easurable, or quantifiable
- **A**chievable, within the contexts and resources available
- **R**elevant, in that they contribute to organizational success, and are aligned with corporate objectives, and
- **T**imely, so that actions are taken at the right time to achieve market success; this involves judging market readiness.

Quantifying objectives makes evaluation easier because it provides specific targets and standards of performance against which outcomes can be measured. It also encourages much more precise thinking about objectives, and is likely to produce more specific objectives. For example, the objective 'to raise awareness of the small-business information service amongst local business' is a broad objective, but the generation of objectives which embed quantifiable measures requires consideration of:

- the specific market sectors in which awareness is to be raised, for example industry sectors, job roles;
- the measures of raised awareness to be used, for example more enquiries, more businesses registered for the service, or more individuals citing the service as a useful source of information when surveyed;
- how large an increase in these awareness measures is required;
- the likely impact on any competitors, and how this could be measured.

## MARKETING STRATEGIES

A marketing strategy is the means by which an organization seeks to achieve its marketing objectives. The main areas of focus are the definition of the target market and the marketing mix to be employed, including key messages and channels to be exploited. Chapter 3 explored the issues associated with target markets and the segmentation of customers. The choice of segments is influenced by the competitive structure of the market, and thus by the competitors' various roles in the marketplace. The issue of competitive positioning has been explored earlier in this chapter. Typically the organization has a range of strategic options which support the achievement of its objectives. Some of these will be related to increasing volume, whilst others will relate to improving profitability in existing market segments. Typical options in this last category include: reducing costs; increasing prices; streamlining operations; and changing the product mix. The key feature of marketing strategy is that it offers a clear statement of the basis for differentiation from competitors.

> REFLECT: Choose an information product or service with which you are associated, and identify the basis on which it differs from its competitors.

## MARKETING PROGRAMMES

This stage is concerned with the detailed implementation of marketing strategies. The marketing programme specifies precisely actions, responsibilities and time-scales. Actions are outlined by market segment, product and functional area. Within the marketing programme, each mix element is considered individually, in contrast to the marketing strategy in which the integration and synergy between these elements is emphasized. The programme must propose a marketing mix that is affordable, implementable and appropriate for the target market.

## MARKETING BUDGETS

A clear statement of the expenditure necessary to deliver the portfolio of marketing activities outlined in the plan is essential. Costs identified in such a budget are likely to include those associated with promotion, marketing research, sales force training, and distribution channel development. The cost of marketing activity relative to the anticipated effect on sales or service delivery is often a significant constraint on the choice of medium used.

The budget is frequently a sticking point in many planning processes. Senior management need to agree both budgets and other elements of the plan, but it is not uncommon for a plan to be rejected on the basis of limitations on available resources. Absence of budget approval will often require the planner to review the earlier stages in the planning cycle; tactics must be adopted to avoid too many repetitions of this process, which can undermine the ability to set a clear plan and to ensure a wide awareness of, and commitment to, the plan.

## IMPLEMENTATION OF THE MARKETING PLAN

Implementation of the plan involves delivering the actions associated with it, as discussed throughout the other chapters in this book. Schedules specifying activities are necessary to ensure that there is a shared understanding of the activities through which the plan is to be implemented.

## CONTROLS AND EVALUATION

Finally, it is necessary to establish how the outcome of any marketing activity can be evaluated, and where the responsibility for that evaluation will lie. The processes associated with matching outcomes to projections and objectives must be documented. Evaluation includes that of individual marketing activities, culminating in an annual review of progress in meeting marketing objectives. Although an annual review offers an opportunity to take an overview, progress towards objectives should also be monitored over shorter periods of, say, one or three months. Failure to achieve interim targets should provoke a review of elements of the marketing plan. The knowledge-based organization will use this evaluation process and the reports that emanate from it as the basis for learning about strengths and weaknesses, effective promotional strategies, the quality of their relationships with specific target markets, and the benefits that are sought by customers in specific segments. Feedback from being in a marketplace is a very powerful, but high-risk, form of marketing research.

The sections to be included in a marketing plan are listed in Figure 10.10.

## CONCLUSION

This chapter has briefly reviewed some key issues and models in the areas of marketing strategy and marketing planning. Marketing strategies are formulated by organizations in order to achieve competitive advantage. A prerequisite of this is an understanding of the industry structure. Porter's model of competitive forces and the comparative advantage model can be helpful in offering appropriate insights into industry structures. Cost-structure-based analysis is a further approach. Competitor analysis focuses on the marketing strategy of individual competitors. The Boston Consulting Group Matrix is a useful tool in assessing

1. Executive summary, indicating key points and directions.
2. Introduction, providing the context against which the plan may be constructed. Content might refer to key achievements from earlier marketing activities, competitor position or marketplace development.
3. Marketing audit, which reviews the marketing position of the organization, and in particular identifies opportunities for future development.
4. Marketing objectives, which in the context of corporate objectives identifies the achievements that are sought through the marketing plan.
5. Marketing strategies, which identifies key strategic options that are to be pursued. If appropriate, this section may be integrated with the next section, on marketing programmes.
6. Marketing programmes and implementation, which specifies in some detail the specific actions, responsibilities and timescales to be undertaken during the period of the plan. This section might also indicate how the success of marketing initiatives is to be evaluated.
7. Marketing budget, which indicates the resources necessary to implement the marketing plan.

**Figure 10.10**   Practical tips on the sections in a marketing plan

product portfolios in terms of their cost structures. All of these models are only offered as frameworks to help in analysing competition, by focusing competitor and industry analysis on factors that are relevant in establishing competitive advantage.

Guidelines have been offered for the stages in the marketing planning process and the sections in a marketing plan. Marketing planning for even a modest commitment of resources (even if these cannot be identified separately, they are embedded in the delivery of a service or other activities in the organization) must include the identification of marketing objectives and those activities necessary to the achievement of marketing objectives. The activities must also be evaluated.

# Index

193